Acknowledgement

With special thanks to Pam, Barry, Ernest, Leslie, Neil and Alec and everyone else who so kindly contributed to this book.

I would also like to thank my editor Rosemary for her unfailing patience, good advice and constant encouragement.

Bettina Luxon 1988

Contents

Chapter One: On The Right Lines 9

Chapter Two: Assessing Your Business Potential 17

Have you got what it takes to succeed in business? Hand shapes. The business hand-shake. Individual fingers. The thumb.

Chapter Three: The Vital Qualities 34

Energy. Concentration. Determination. Confidence. Holly's story.

Chapter Four: Will You Be A Success? 42

Success line. George's story. Fiona's story.

Chapter Five: Will You Make A Million 55

Sally's story. Managing millions. Running the Royal Family firm.

Chapter Six: The Hand Which Means Business 67

Famous business hands.

Chapter Seven: Are You Good At Decision Making? 81

Philip's story. Intuition. Running the country.

Chapter Eight: Have You Got The Killer Instinct? 90

Ruthlessness. Charm. Persuasiveness. Vic's story.

Chapter Nine: Assessing Your Job Potential ... 96

Pamela's story. Shaping up. Tracey's story.

Chapter Ten: Choosing Your Career 105

Suitable careers. Writer. Dentist. Engineer. Stockbroker. Investment banker. Beautician. Accountancy. Lawyer. Actors and actresses. Artists.

Chapter Eleven: Appointing The Right Staff   114

Checklist for choosing staff. Building a team. How to spot a conman. Motivating force. Are you a good boss?

Chapter Twelve: Should You Go Into Partnership? 126

Successful partners. Types to avoid in any form of business.

Chapter Thirteen: Should You Diversify? 143

Will you recover from a setback? The overseas connection. Ian's story.

Chapter Fourteen: Stress 154

Stress grilles. Self-induced worry. Personality factors.

Chapter Fifteen: How To Combine Home With Business 160

The workaholic. The balanced approach. Partners in stress.

Index 171

CHAPTER ONE:
ON THE RIGHT LINES

It was the worst time of John Fletcher's life. He had recently gone into partnership and regretted it almost at once. Now his business prospects looked poor, money was tight, his confidence and optimism deserted him. A shrewd down-to-earth businessman dealing in stocks and shares. John Fletcher is not given to impulsive behaviour, but on this occasion he needed help. He contacted palmist Bettina Luxon.

> 'My sister in law had been to her several times with very good results' said John, 'and she gave me the idea. I was desperate. I didn't know where I was going in life.'

John Fletcher had four meetings with Bettina over the next few years and was amazed by her predictions.

> 'She knew nothing about me but she was able to tell me at once that I was unhappy in a partnership and that the partner was no good. When the partner goes things will change for the better, she said. She went on to say that I would form a new partnership with two men — she even gave me the initials of their names — and that this would be the start of something very good. "You are going to make a lot of money and once you get started things will improve dramatically," she said.

'Bettina added that the first major deal we made would occur nine or ten months after the partnership was formed. She was absolutely right on all counts.

'My first partner was not a good man. For legal reasons it took me six months to get out of that entanglement. My former partner is now bankrupt and no longer living in the country. I went on to form a new partnership with two other men (even the initials were right!) and the business immediately improved. Then ten months later we pulled off a major deal which really set us up.'

When John Fletcher met Bettina she had also given him a lot of personal information which was absolutely correct but she'd added that he would be moving to his dream house. At the time money was in such short supply that John Fletcher found this difficult to believe. Yet as things improved he did go on to buy a beautiful house.

'Strangely enough Bettina even said I was psychic and that this ability helped me in business. I don't know about that, but although I'm not an impulsive person I do sometimes wake up in the morning with the gut feeling that it's time to sell and 99% of the time I'm right. That first major deal ten months into my new partnership was just such a case. I decided it was right to sell and I sold at a price that I don't think will ever be obtained again.'

John Fletcher finds all this somewhat bemusing. He doesn't know how Bettina does it, but he is in no doubt as to the help she gave him. Writing to her recently about the 'uncanny' accuracy of her predictions he ended his letter:

'. . . In conclusion I must emphasise a number of points. At no time did you have any knowledge of my financial or domestic situation. Your forecasts were made when I was at my lowest ebb and could then have only been believed by a super-optimist. You gave me renewed hope and from then on everything just escalated.'

John Fletcher is no starry-eyed crank. He is an astute businessman, but Bettina's skill left him with unanswered questions. He said:

'In my mind there is no rational explanation for all this!'

Well, it may not be rational but the explanation is obvious and simple. It is not yet clear why, but to a palmist the hand is a map of the future and once you know the signs to look for you really can make out the shape of things to come. You can go further. Simply by looking at the shape and texture of a person's hands and fingers you can learn a great deal about their character before they've even opened their mouth.

Bettina Luxon has been a palmist for the last 25 years and she has been studying hands since early childhood. She is the first to admit that experience is invaluable.

'You don't have to be psychic to read palms,' she says, 'anyone can do it. There are rules that can be learned. But the more you do, the more your psychic abilities develop. A beginner wouldn't have been able to see the initials of John Fletcher's new partners for instance, that was my psychic ability taking over, but a beginner would have been able to forecast simply from the lines on his palm, that John was going to form a new partnership with two people and that it would succeed.'

We still don't really understand why palmistry works but it is a fact that no two hands are the same, no two

11

palm prints are the same and no palm stays the same throughout life. As a person's life changes, so the lines on their palm change. New lines appear and disappear all the time, reflecting changing circumstances.

Like most palmists, Bettina Luxon gets impatient with people who dismiss palmistry as some sort of old fashioned superstition. She believes that palmistry is a science, the study of which can be very useful in the modern world.

'Already we're seeing enlighted individuals from all walks of life — medicine, the police force, business — taking an interest in palmistry,' she explained. 'In business it is particularly useful. Studying your palm will help you make all sorts of decisions, whether to go into partnership or not, whether you should change direction, whether you are in the right business at all and so on. Equally important, it will also help you to assess other people.'

Sometimes a businessman will have to come to a decision about a person he has only just met. Now we all have instincts about new people but most of us can be taken in at times by surface charm and an impressive exterior. This is where palmistry can help. You don't have to start holding hands with a stranger! If you know what you're looking for, a glance at the person's hands as he reaches for a coffee cup, picks up a paper, takes out a cigarette — will give you all sorts of clues to his true character.

When John Fletcher first came to visit her, Bettina examined his hands under a good light.

'I saw at once that his palms were covered in a network of tiny lines like little grilles,' she recalled. 'This is a sure sign of stress. I also noticed that there were islands in the line I call the success line (sometimes known as the fate line). This is another sign of stress showing that it is connected with the person's career and that he would be well advised to take a break.' (See Fig 1[a])

'John's success line started at the wrist with two branches that merged together into one line. This told me that he was in partnership but almost immediately after the branches merged, the success line began to fade. I realised at once that John's problems were connected with his partner.'

'This of course wasn't a good sign but beyond the islands the success line went on clear and strong to end under the third finger which indicates achievement in business. What's more another faint success line was beginning on the headline and tracing it's way up to the base of the first finger which means that things should go well financially. I realised that John would do very well in his business providing he overcame his present problems.'

John Fletcher was pretty impressed with this interpretation but Bettina was able to go further. By studying his fingers she could tell that he had the necessary mental qualities to surmount his difficulties.

'How did I know? Well his fingers were straight and the phalanges were equal. This shows a well balanced, reasonable personality, capable of clear, analytical thought. The first phalange at the top of his thumb was well developed indicating a very strong will. It was quite obvious that John had the mental powers to discover the solution to his problems and the determination to put that solution into practice.

13

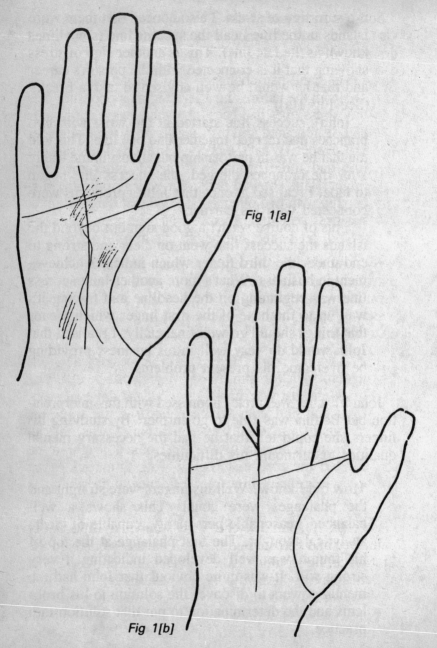

Fig 1[a]

Fig 1[b]

Some months later John Fletcher paid Bettina another visit. She saw at once that his life had improved dramatically. (See Fig 1[b])

'His hand had changed,' said Bettina, 'as you can see from the before and after diagrams opposite. The tiny stress lines had been smoothed away, the islands had disappeared and his success lines were stronger and deeper. What's more one branch of his success line had three prongs and ended under the little finger. This showed that John was going into partnership with two other people and that they had great business potential. I knew that from then on things would get better and better for him.'

By this time John Fletcher had managed to end his first partnership and he was about to join forces with two other men. He never looked back. He is now a wealthy man.

Bettina insists that his current success has nothing to do with her:

'It was all there. He had all the necessary qualities to achieve it for himself and that's what he did. The trouble is that you can get very bogged down in problems and find yourself unable to see the way out. Palmistry can clarify the situation. I was able to reassure John that the future looked bright if he tackled the area that was holding him back. That knowledge gave him the confidence to do what was needed.'

Perhaps if John Fletcher had known a little about palmistry and had studied that bad partner's hands in the first place, he wouldn't have gone into the partnership at all, thus saving himself a lot of headaches.

However, just because palmistry can identify a problem it doesn't always follow that the sufferer will take his palmist's advice. As Bettina explains:

'The hand shows your potential success and warns of difficulties ahead but you can destroy everything by not heeding the warnings. I had a client whose palms showed every success line possible but he also had strong signs of stress and an indication that he was trying to go into too many different fields at once.'

Naturally Bettina warned him to slow down and concentrate his efforts into fewer areas. He didn't. Impossible, he said. The next time she saw him, his business was in ruins. He had lost everything. When Bettina looked at his palm she saw that the success line had completely disappeared.

The following chapters provide a simple introduction to palmistry. Their study won't turn you into an expert palmist overnight. It takes patience and practice. But you will find a great deal of interesting and valuable information which you can start putting to good use at once. Persevere, and you will find that palmistry has a very special place in your business.

CHAPTER TWO:
ASSESSING YOUR BUSINESS POTENTIAL

Imagine setting off to drive across a remote and inhospitable country without bothering to take a map, a compass or to find out whether your car is capable of the journey.

Madness?

Well, in business people do it all the time. They launch themselves into a new venture without the slightest idea of what lies ahead or whether they are suited to the project. Oh they talk to the bank, they research the market and they juggle with the budget if they've got any sense. But they scorn to use a valuable tool which is lying right in front of their noses and which costs nothing at all. The fund of relevant information written in their own hand.

Ridiculous?

Well, I believe that after assembling all the conventional facts, your hand can supply you with everything else you need to know about whether your business will be a success, how you should run it and if you should be in it at all.

Hard to believe?

Well, why not read on and put my theories to the test.

Have you got what it takes to succeed in business?

Every successful businessman is different. Some claw

their way from barrow boy to captain of industry, others inherit wealth and steer the family firm to ever greater heights. Some have degrees from the best universities, others leave school without a GCE to their name. Their tastes and interests are as diverse as the pebbles on a beach. Yet no matter what their backgrounds or education, time and time again you find that successful businessmen and women share certain fundamental characteristics.

When you look at their hands the same is true. Every palm is different. No two people have exactly the same configuration of lines. Yet while the details of their personalities and lives are different successful businessmen and women also share common characteristics and these characteristics can be seen in the shape of their hands and fingers.

I don't think I've ever come across a successful businessman with the 'wrong' type of hand shape for instance. I'm not saying it's impossible to succeed if your hand is a certain shape — many other factors have to be taken into consideration — but it must be an uphill struggle. I remember one woman who came to see me. She was trying to make a success of an antiques business. At least she thought she was trying to make a success of it.

> 'I can't understand it,' she said 'I've got some very nice pieces but at the end of the month I don't seem to have made any money.'

One glance at her hands was enough to explain the problem. They were slender and pointed. Very attractive to look at with well manicured and polished nails, but hopeless as far as business was concerned. People with such hands are more interested in beauty than in money and it soon became clear that although this woman had indeed stocked her shop with some very good antiques, she didn't want to sell them. Unconsciously she was sabotaging her own business because she didn't want to let her lovely things go.

Palmists usually divide hands into four basic shapes; spatulate, conical, square and pointed. (See Figs 2[a], [b], [c] and [d]) Simply by studying the outline of the hand you can discover the 'outline' of the personality. It is quite common to have a mixed hand with characteristics from two or more of the main types. So study your hands and those you wish to analyse with care. (See Fig 2[e])

One word of caution before you get started. Palmistry is not a simple science. I'm still learning after more than 25 years of study. You need to remember that various aspects in the hand can have more than one interpretation. A long first finger for instance can indicate leadership qualities or it can show an arrogant, domineering nature. It all depends whether mainly positive or mainly negative traits predominate in the rest of the hand. So be patient and don't jump to conclusions.

We describe in brief the key features of each of the five types of hands and give them a business rating, the top score being five stars ★ ★ ★ ★ ★.

The spatulate hand

The spatulate hand has a large, broad palm with thick, blunt fingers widening slightly at the tips to resemble a spatula. The palm is often hard and unyielding rather than springy in texture. The owners of such hands are people of action, often excelling in sport. Original and unconventional they are often very courageous. Explorers and navigators have spatulate hands, so have some of our greatest painters.

Ambitious and independent these people prefer to work on their own ideas rather than those of others. They are often executives, and administrators. Energetic in business

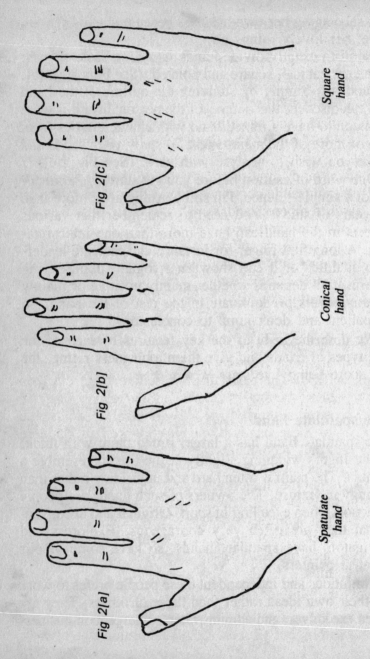

Fig 2[a]

Fig 2[b]

Fig 2[c]

Spatulate hand

Conical hand

Square hand

they make good partners. Millionaires often have this type of hand.
Business rating: ★ ★ ★ ★ ★

The conical hand

The conical hand has a long palm which tapers slightly towards to the top. The fingers are full at the base and slightly pointed at the tip with long nails. Moody, emotional and impulsive the owners of such hands can be rather unstable personalities. At their worst they can be quick tempered and selfish. At their best they are generous and sympathetic.

These people are plodders in their careers and more likely to give money away than to make it. They are not usually good in business.
Business rating: ★

The square hand

The square hand is the most common shape found in all walks of life. The palm forms a square from the wrist to the base of the fingers. Ambitious and law-abiding with a respect for authority and a methodical approach, the owners of these hands often do very well in business. Lawyers and accountants possess square hands.

Since this is such a common hand shape it is necessary to examine the fingers as well for a more accurate analysis. When the square hand is accompanied by small fingers, this indicates a person who does not like responsibility even though he is likely to make money. These people much prefer to be self-employed and should avoid partnerships.
Business rating: ★ ★ ★

When the square hand is accompanied by long fingers with knotty joints (Robert Maxwell has this type of hand)

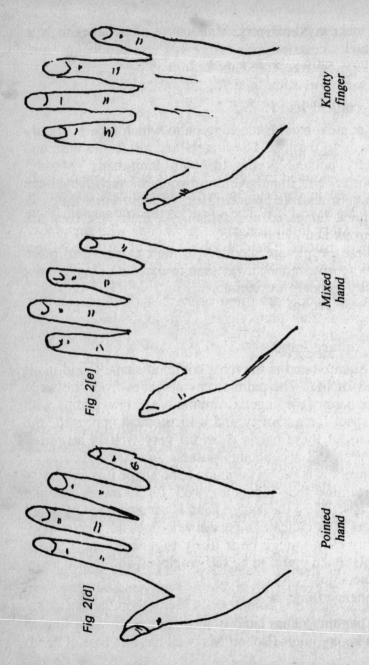

Knotty
finger

Mixed
hand

Pointed
hand

Fig 2[e]

Fig 2[d]

it shows great enterprise and a love of detail though a tendency to cautiousness at times. These people are hard working, often reserved and once they have made a decision they will stick to it till the bitter end.

Business rating ★ ★ ★ ★

The pointed hand

Long and pointed in appearance this is the type of hand often seen in flattering portraits of the past but rarely occurring in real life. The owner of the true pointed hand loves beauty in all things and can't cope with mundane, practical matters. They have little idea of thrift and often fail to make provision for the future.

Usually gifted in some way and with a vivid imagination these people are often painters, writers of verse or composers. They are not good in business and are seldom found there.

Business rating: ★

The mixed hand

Sometimes a hand does not fit easily into any of these categories but contains elements of all four. The owners of these hands could be called 'Jacks of all Trades'. They have potential in many areas but somehow fail to make a success in material terms, in any.

Brilliant engineers, inventors and research workers often have this type of hand. Clever and analytical they are more interested in the task they have chosen for themselves than in material success. They will devote themselves exclusively to the work in hand but then lose interest when it is completed. Often others benefit from their labours. They are not usually good in business.

Business rating: ★

23

The business hand-shake

Like many cliches, the one about the firm hand-shake denoting an honest, trustworthy character is largely true. Such a hand-shake can sometimes be faked on a first meeting of course, but once the person is relaxed they are likely to revert to their true type. Most people's hand-shakes fall easily into one of three categories:

1. Generally, a limp, soft hand is indicative of an indolent mind and an easy conscience. If the hand is flabby as well it reflects a highly sensuous nature.
   Business rating: ★

2. An elastic but firm grip points to mental and physical strength, honesty and an intuitive and alert mind.
   Business rating: ★ ★ ★ ★ ★

3. If the grip is like iron and the hand very hard, it shows great energy and strength of will verging on ruthlessness. In extreme cases there is a possibility of cruelty.
   Business rating: ★ ★ — ★ ★ ★ ★ ★ (depends on whether all that energy is suitably directed)

The fingers

Once you have discovered your hand shape or the shape of the person you are studying, you will have established a broad outline of the personality. Now you can begin to shade in the details and the next step is to look at the fingers. Generally speaking, short fingers show an energetic, quick thinking individual, inclined to impatience. These fingers belong to the type of person who likes to think big but cannot be bothered with tiresome details.

24

Long fingers reflect a patient, slower paced person who takes time to come to decisions and will go to great lengths to get details right. Critical and analytical of thought these people will not be swayed by the opinions of others.

Straight, close-set fingers hint of a stiff, intolerant nature with a tendency to meanness. Fingers which are wider spread show a more open temperament and when the fingers are set well apart it indicates a generous easy-going nature. Ideally all the phalanges of the fingers (the three joints) should be the same length, indicating a well balanced nature.

It is worth looking at the line created at the base of the fingers where they join the palm. If the first three fingers (excluding the little finger) form a near enough straight line it shows an even temper and balanced personality. I have often found this formation in the hands of very successful people.

Where the fingers slope away and the little finger is set low on the hand, it shows that the owner of this hand will have to achieve material success through his own efforts. Should this finger be set excessively low, it suggests an uphill struggle all the way. When people are born to wealth, all four fingers on their hand are usually set in a straight line. (See Figs 2[f] and 2 [g])

Individual fingers

To avoid confusion, palmists have given each finger it's own name. The first finger or index finger is known as **Jupiter**. The second finger **Saturn**. The third finger or ring finger is called **Apollo** and the fourth finger or little finger, **Mercury**. The length of each finger is measured against that of the second finger of Saturn. Traditionally, each finger has it's own area of influence in life. Fig 2[h] will help you identify the individual fingers correctly.

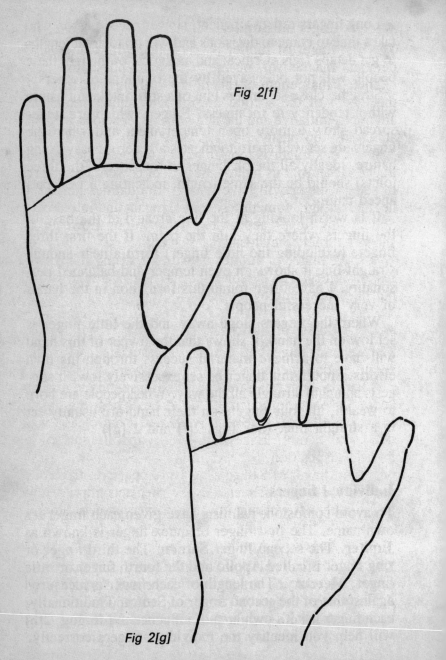

Fig 2[f]

Fig 2[g]

● The finger of Jupiter

The first finger of Jupiter is associated with leadership, personal magnetism, business acumen and status.

The normal length of this finger is about four fifths of the length of the second finger. This shows moderate ambition, initiative and the ability to be tenacious without appearing too pushy.

When this finger is long (almost as long as the second finger of Saturn) this indicates a love of power. The owner of such a finger will have leadership qualities although he or she might sometimes seem arrogant and intolerant. Should this finger appear excessively long however it shows a cruel, dictatorial nature.

A short finger of Jupiter suggests a strong dislike of responsibility. The person with this type of finger would not be happy employing staff.

● The finger of Saturn

The second finger of Saturn is associated with the emotions and mental and physical powers.

A normal finger of Saturn indicates a sound judgement and a reasoned approach to problems. When this finger is long it tells of a love of solitude and a more cautious, deliberate nature. Excessively long and it hints of a morbid disposition.

A short finger of Saturn shows an impulsive, frivolous nature. The owner of such a finger often acts imprudently and is better off working under the supervision of others.

● The finger of Apollo

The third finger of Apollo, the lucky sun finger is associated with the arts, talent, fame and fortune.

The normal length of the finger of Apollo, the ring finger is about nine-tenths that of the second finger. This type of finger indicates a person who is prepared to take

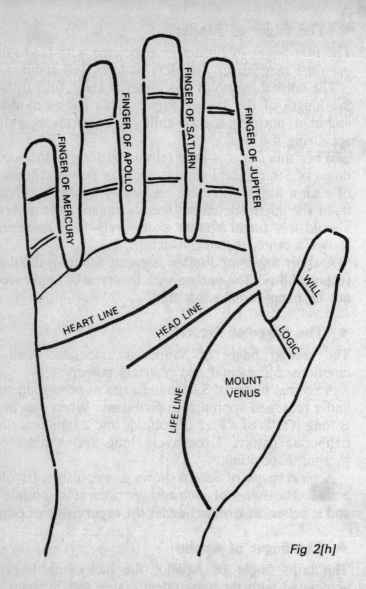

FINGER OF MERCURY

FINGER OF APOLLO

FINGER OF SATURN

FINGER OF JUPITER

HEART LINE

HEAD LINE

WILL

LOGIC

LIFE LINE

MOUNT VENUS

Fig 2[h]

a calculated risk. He is never foolhardy but neither is he over cautious.

A long finger of Apollo suggests a gambler. The owner of such a finger is willing to risk everything in order to gain more. Sometimes this pays off. Often it leads to disaster.

A short finger of Apollo tells of muddled thinking and indecisiveness.

● The finger of Mercury

The little finger of Mercury is associated with ambition, business, and financial matters.

The normal length for the finger of Mercury, the little finger is reckoned by be seven tenths the length of the second finger. Such a finger denotes tact, adaptability and a flexible approach.

A long finger of Mercury is a very good sign for the businessman, suggesting drive, ambition and leadership qualities. The owner of such a finger is usually very articulate. Excessively long however and there is a tendency to deceitfulness.

A short finger of Mercury indicates a quarrelsome, rather hasty nature.

● The thumb

The thumb is the most important digit on the hand. It indicates intellect, will-power and the exercise of that will-power. Often a person with 'weak' fingers will have a strong thumb and this helps them correct and overcome their more negative qualities. A strong thumb found on a hand with strong fingers heightens all the positive qualities. Conversely, a weak thumb found on an otherwise strong hand will have a detrimental effect.

29

It is interesting to note that in it's first few weeks of life a baby is completely dependent on others. It sleeps much of the time and gets very little chance to exercise it's intellect or will and it's thumb is tucked tightly inside the hand with the fingers closed over it. As the baby develops a will of it's own, so the thumb comes out of it's hiding place.

A thumb set well down on the hand similar to a chimpanzee's, indicates lack of intellect. Normally when the thumb is held close to the first finger of Jupiter it reaches the first joint or just below it. Should it reach beyond the first joint it is known as a long thumb. Well below this and it's a short thumb.

Generally a long thumb indicates strength of character and a person who is ruled by the head rather than the heart. Short thumbs tend to belong to day-dreamers, talkers rather than doers.

When studying the thumb several points have to be taken into consideration, the flexibility and also the proportions of the phalanges or joints. Fig 2[i] will help guide you.

● The inflexible thumb

This thumb is straight and firm and the top joint does not bend back away from the hand even when pressed. This denotes a reliable, generous nature but not a 'soft touch'. Owners of firm thumbs are not easily put upon, neither are they impulsive where money is concerned. They have to guard against narrow mindedness.

Should such a thumb be accompanied by a coarse, leathery skin the subject is likely to be mean and unsympathetic.

● The flexible thumb

This thumb is supple and arched, the top joint bending

30

back away from the hand. This denotes an impulsive nature. Should the thumb bend back from the nail joint the owner is gregarious, adaptable and flexible in outlook.

When the top joint of this type of thumb is rather thick it shows a nature determined to the point of awkwardness if crossed.

● The first phalange

The first or top phalange indicates the degree of will power and determination. When this joint is overdeveloped it is a sure sign of obstinacy. When it is thin and insignificant it shows lack of stability and will power. Owners of these thumbs are easily bullied.

● The second phalange

The second joint of the thumb which is often waisted in appearance indicates intelligence and reasoning powers. Ideally it should be the same length as the first joint since intelligence without determination is likely to be wasted and determination without intelligence gets you nowhere.

A long second phalange to the thumb in a hand with long, straight fingers shows a person who is utterly trustworthy and devoted to detail.

When the second phalange is excessively waisted it shows tact and diplomacy but also great cunning. You can never quite trust the owner of such a thumb and they are best avoided in business.

● The murderer's thumb

This type of thumb doesn't necessarily belong to a murderer of course but it does indicate a potentially violent nature. It is very easy to recognise. The thumb is short and the first phalange is overdeveloped to the point of bulbousness. The owner of such a thumb is dangerously obstinate with a quick temper and can be violent when

31

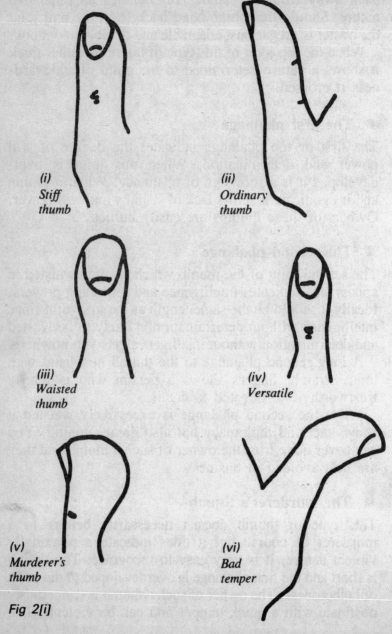

(i)
*Stiff
thumb*

(ii)
*Ordinary
thumb*

(iii)
*Waisted
thumb*

(iv)
Versatile

(v)
*Murderer's
thumb*

(vi)
*Bad
temper*

Fig 2[i]

upset. At best, such types have to work hard to keep their temper under control. At worst, they are capable of murder.

A few years ago I saw just such a thumb. A distressed mother begged me to look at her son's hand. It was obvious that the boy was something of a problem and when I looked at his hand it was very difficult to find anything comforting to say.

His thumb was set well down, almost like an ape's and it was short and heavy with an ugly bulbous tip. The boy had a very low IQ and was subject to such violent fits of temper that at times his mother couldn't control him and had to call in psychiatric help. Sadly, the lad didn't have the intelligence to curb his moods and he would probably end up in an institution. I must stress, however, that this type of thumb is thankfully quite rare.

CHAPTER THREE:
THE VITAL QUALITIES

The young man sitting before me had great plans he said. He was going to start his own business, expand rapidly, explore the overseas market. Why in no time at all he would be a millionaire. I smiled non-commitally and picked up his hand. It was an unusual shape, particularly for a man. Thin and narrow, almost like a dog's paw. It was not the shape I'd expect to find in a successful businessman but as I explained in the last chapter, there are many other points to be taken into consideration and I peered more closely at the young man's palm.

His headline was short, his thumb weak . . . everywhere I looked there were negative aspects. It soon became clear that this man would never run the business of his dreams. That's all it was — a dream. He had plans but he simply didn't have the necessary qualities to bring them to fruition.

Examine any group of successful businessmen and women and you soon notice that they are not necessarily the people with the most original or the greatest number of ideas. In fact at times their ideas seem downright obvious. 'I could have thought of that,' we often say in amazement when reading of some new business venture that has unexpectedly taken off breaking all records. Yet these golden men and women succeed where other more apparently creative thinkers fail.

Why? Well it's not luck, though good luck certainly

helps. What these people share are certain vital characteristics without which they would be unable to put even the most brilliant ideas into practice. Extrovert or introvert, intellectual or 'salt of the earth' they all possess the same qualities.

These qualities can be plainly seen in the hand. Fig 3[a] shows the main lines to look for and it is important to remember that a right-handed person should read from the right as his left hand shows his past, a left-handed person should read from the left as his right hand shows his past.

If you are reading your own palm it will probably be easier to make a print of it (the simplest way is to place your hand on a photocopying machine and take a copy. You will be surprised at how well the main lines show up) since if you try to do it 'in the flesh' you'll be working upside down. Hands are usually read from the finger-tips down rather than from the wrist up.

● **Energy**

It takes a great deal of energy to get a new business off the ground and it takes enormous stamina to maintain and improve an existing venture in today's competitive market. Without sufficient energy, the potential businessman will tire too quickly to achieve his aims and if he fails to heed the warnings his body is giving him, he could even damage his health in the struggle to the top.

High energy is shown in a reddish palm, strongly marked, highly coloured lines and probably a firm texture to the hand. Spatula handshapes contain the most energy — many athletes have spatula hands — followed by square hands and the harder the hand, the more energy is available. Soft, flabby hands suggest the type of person who has plenty of ideas but no stamina to carry them through.

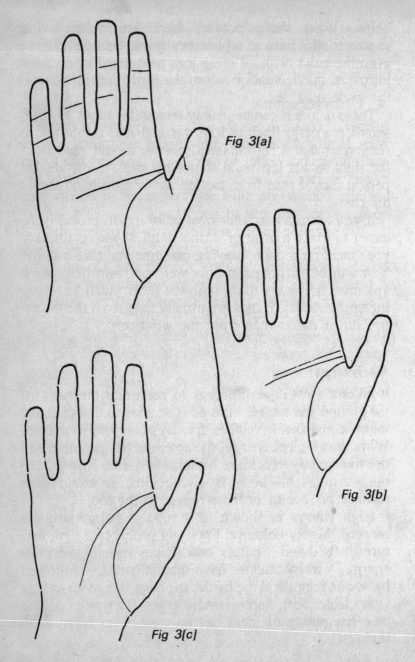

Fig 3[a]

Fig 3[b]

Fig 3[c]

Pallid hands with pale, faintly marked lines often belong to people who have to rely on others and need to delegate a great deal.

● **Concentration**

Energy of course is absolutely necessary, but the energetic person can dash around from project to project, starting many things but failing to carry them through. The ability to concentrate on one task at a time and single-mindedly see it to completion must also be present if energy is to be harnessed and put to good use.

Concentration and all forms of mental powers show in the headline (see Fig 3[b], and [c]). Ideally this line should be deep and strong, slightly sloping and not too short. A headline like this is indicative of concentration, inteligence and shrewdness in financial matters. When the headline is short, reaching barely to the second finger of Saturn it suggests poor concentration and weak mental powers. A long headline is a sign of an excellent memory.

It is very important to look at the slope of the headline too. Sometimes this line doesn't appear to slope at all. It marches across the hand straight as a ruler. This isn't a bad sign in business because it shows someone who puts work before pleasure every time, but it can cause problems in private life. When the headline slopes morc steeply, great imagination is present but should it drop away right down into the hand it indicates a tendency to depression.

Occasionally another line runs parallel to the headline, just beneath it. This is known as a double headline and is a very good sign. The owner of such a headline is likely to be very clever.

● **Determination**

To energy, concentration and intellect, the potential

businessman needs to add determination if he hopes to succeed. I mentioned luck earlier. To a certain extent we all make our own luck. As I believe a top golfer once said 'It's funny, the more I practise the luckier I get.' This is quite true, but I believe it is also true that good and bad luck sometimes occur for no apparent reason.

The shrewd businessman will of course capitalise on any good luck that comes his way but he will also have to contend at times with bad luck. I doubt if there is any businessman in the world no matter how successful, who has never had to cope with a bad patch. It happens to everyone. The difference between success and failure however is often the ability to grit your teeth and battle on through difficult times, until every obstacle has been overcome.

Many people with otherwise great potential have come unstuck because they simply didn't have the determination to weather the storms. The determined person will have a strong thumb with a well developed first phalange and probably firm fingertips as well. Coupled with a good headline this is the ideal combination for a businessman.

Should the first phalange be markedly longer than the second it shows obstinacy bordering on mulishness at times — not necessarily a helpful trait. When the first phalange is short and thin it denotes lack of willpower and is often found in the hands of people who have been the victims of bullies.

● Confidence

It is surprising how many people possess all the qualities mentioned, yet lack confidence. With so many gifts they ought to be brimming over with self assurance and yet for some reason they are not. Lack of confidence is not necessarily a disaster for a businessman, particularly if he has great determination to make up for it, but it is a handicap and can hold him back at times.

Like the firm handshake, surface confidence can be faked, for a while, but nothing can beat the peace of mind that comes with natural assurance. You don't even need to look at a person's hand to see whether they are confident or not. If they walk along, head high, arms swinging, hands loose and comfortable, they are confident. Fingers tucked into a fist shows nervousness.

However, confidence is also written in the palm. (See Figs 3[d] and [e]) If the headline begins separate from the lifeline it indicates a confident, independent nature. This is heightened if the little finger of Mercury is a good length, not too long and not too short. An overlong finger of Mercury reaching up almost to the tip of the third finger suggests overconfidence which could lead to trouble.

If the lifeline and headline are joined together at the start it suggests lack of confidence and a dependence on the subject's family. The sooner the lines separate the greater the confidence and independence.

Holly's story

Having started this chapter with an example of a young man who did not possess these vital qualities and therefore never did get a business off the ground despite his dreams, I thought I'd end with the story of a woman who had a perfect business hand — and did not know it. Holly worked in a hairdresser's shop and had studied hard to pass her exams. A bright young woman she sensed that life held more for her than marriage to the boy next door and a mundane nine to five job and she came to me to see if there were better things in store.

Holly's hands were slightly discoloured by hair dye, but there was no mistaking the potential written in them. Square and capable, the lines strongly marked showing energy. Holly's first finger of Jupiter was almost as long

39

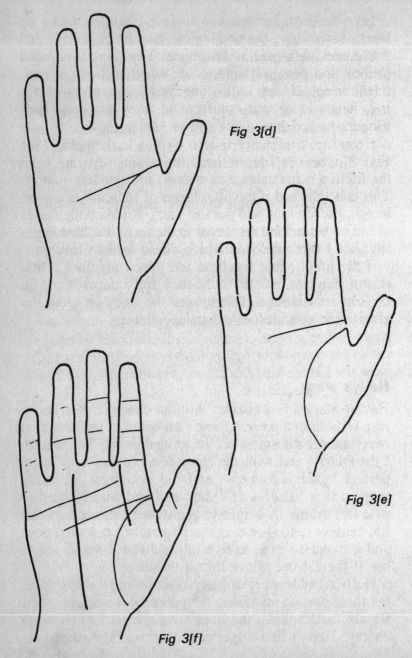

Fig 3[d]

Fig 3[e]

Fig 3[f]

as her second finger, indicating that she wouldn't be happy working for someone else for long.

The first and second phalanges of her thumb were even, denoting intellect and willpower. What's more there was a bold ambition line striking out across her palm and a clear success line. (See Fig 3[f]) Holly had the tenacity, the drive and ambition to start her own business. She had the necessary mental powers as well as the natural businesswoman's square hand. She was clearly heading for success.

'You know you ought to be self employed,' I told her.

'I've been thinking about it Bettina,' she admitted, 'but I don't know if I can afford to leave my job.'

'Well if you do, you'll be a success,' I said.

Holly proved me right. Such was her determination that after working in the salon all day, she spent her evenings visiting private clients at home in order to build up capital. It wasn't long before Holly opened her first salon. Now she has a chain and she is expanding into the health and beauty market too.

CHAPTER FOUR:
WILL YOU BE A SUCCESS?

Not long ago I was watching TV and I saw an interview with the best-selling romantic novelist Barbara Cartland. A grand old lady, she was confident and awe-inspiring in her trade-mark pink clothes, her beautifully coiffed platinum hair and her glamorous false eyelashes. Barbara Cartland had panache and I sat down to enjoy her forthright comments.

But a palmist is never off duty, not even when relaxing in front of the TV and without stopping to think I found my gaze dropping from the Cartland features to the hands resting in her lap.

Despite being a writer of escapist romance Ms Cartland's hands were not limp and fey and vague. I was surprised to see that they were large, square and capable with long, but very strong looking fingers and a heavy tip to the thumb (See Fig 4[a]).

She may have looked as sweet as candy floss but this was clearly a woman of enormous strength and character, a woman who would have been very successful in business. That heavy tip to the thumb showed that she wouldn't suffer fools gladly and she could lose her temper quite impressively when provoked.

She also had a very long first finger of Jupiter, almost as long as the second finger of Saturn, indicating a marked ambition to lead. And this was combined with the characteristic knotty finger joints showing a very shrewd mind.

Perhaps when Ms Cartland began her career back in

the nineteen twenties, writing fiction was one of the few avenues open to well-bred young ladies. But had she been starting out today I wouldn't have been surprised to see her end up as a formidable captain of industry. Nevertheless she has made a spectacular success of her writing, showing that her natural talent, steered by her shrewd brain, has been harnessed to the full.

Success line

Unfortunately the cameras didn't permit me a view of Ms Cartland's palms but had they done so I would have expected to see a strong success line running straight up her hand from the base of her wrist to end under the second finger of Saturn.

This is the sort of line you find in a person who has achieved entirely as a result of their own efforts. This person deserves respect because they have worked very very hard for their achievements.

The success line (called by some palmists the fate line, or line of destiny) is a very important indicator of a person's future prospects. Unfortunately it is also quite complicated. For a start not everyone has one. This does not necessarily mean they are doomed to life of failure. It may simply show that they are not concerned with worldly achievements, or, alternatively, that they will have to fight very hard to reach their goal.

If you do not have a success line, however, it is not fixed in position like the life, heart and head lines and it can start and finish in a number of different places – each with their own different meanings. What's more, the line can change, quite rapidly, branching out in different directions or in one case I came across, even disappearing altogether.

The easiest success line to spot is the one like Barbara Cartland's (as I've imagined it) which starts at the base of the hand and travels up the centre of the hand to end under one of the four fingers. Not all success lines behave in this way though. Some start from the head line, others from the

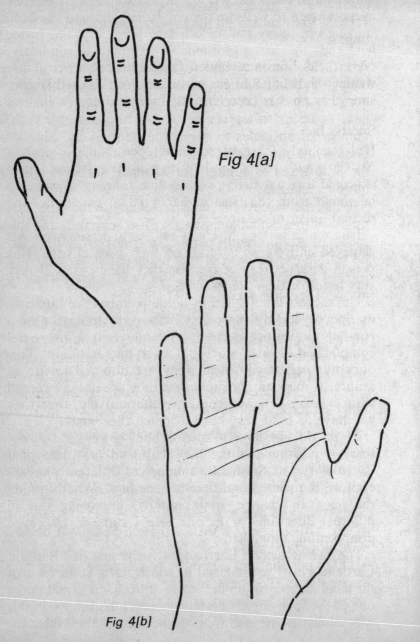

Fig 4[a]

Fig 4[b]

heart line. What they have in common is that they are vertical lines runing up the hand to end under one of the fingers.

A success line is always a good sign but when it ends under the second finger of Saturn (see Fig 4[b]) a few negative aspects creep in. The owner of such a line will have a successful career but it will be a struggle with a number of obstacles to overcome on the way. Should a branch line run off this type of success line to end under the first finger of Jupiter, the eventual succcess will be quite spectacular.

When the success line ends under any of the other three fingers it means that ambitions will be achieved. The third finger of Apollo being particularly lucky. Should a star be visible on the base of this finger either as well as or instead of, a success line, fame and good fortune lie ahead. (See Fig 4[c])

Similarly, should the success line rise strongly through the palm and end under the first finger of Jupiter with a star on the mount the owner will have honour as well as fame. (See Fig 4[d]) I would expect to see this type of line on the hands of somone like Bob Geldof, recently knighted for his work with the starving millions in Africa.

Often I see success lines that chop and change direction with branches shooting out all over the place. This means a number of job changes, or even complete career changes before the ultimate success is reached. (See Fig 4[e])

Sometimes the line will fade for a time, then strengthen again. This suggests a difficult patch ahead but one that will be overcome.

Other people have a number of complete breaks in the success line. The person with such a pattern will face uncertainty in his business and many up and downs. He will need a great deal of determination to fulfil his poten-

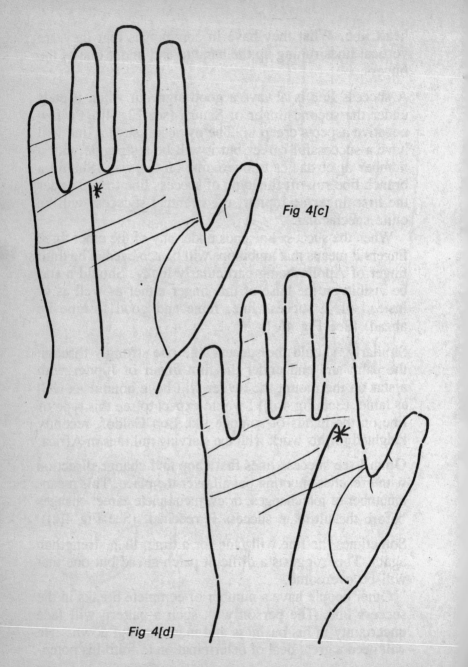

Fig 4[c]

Fig 4[d]

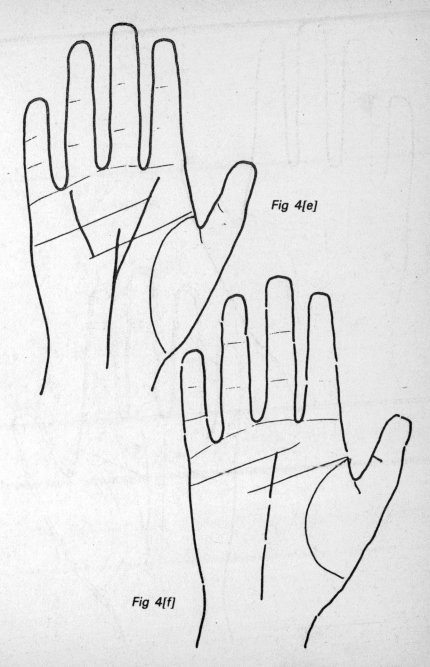

Fig 4[e]

Fig 4[f]

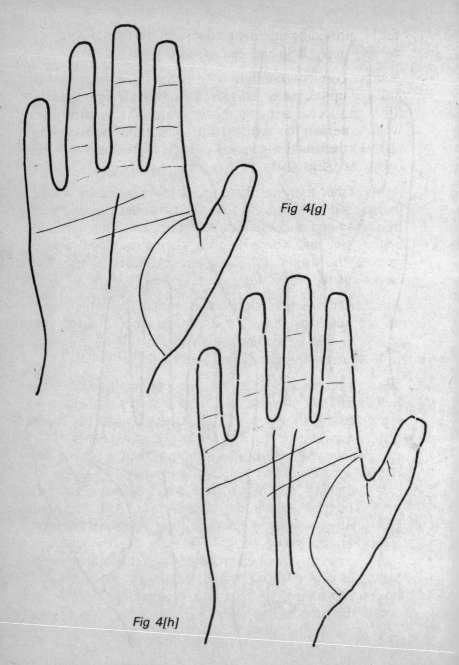

Fig 4[g]

Fig 4[h]

tial but providing the first phalange of his thumb is strong he will make it in the end. (See Fig 4[f])

A more common configuration is the line which begins halfway up the palm. This shows a difficult time in early life with success arriving in later years. This is often seen when a person has worked for some time for someone else and then suddenly leaves and sets up business on their own. (See Fig 4[g])

At the other extreme there are a few rare cases where there is a double success line, the two lines running side by side to end under two different fingers. This is called a sister line and where both lines are strong and clearly marked the owner will have two extremely successful careers at the same time. (See Fig 4[h])

Another common version is the success line which runs up the hand to come to a complete stop, often at the heartline. This means that the owner has run into a barrier in his career and cannot progress. (See Fig 4[i])

There is no need to be too despondent about such a sign however. Once this line has been noticed and the meaning understood the subject can start analysing his situation. Providing he has the other necessary qualities of intelligence and determination he can then work out the reason for the problem and the best way of solving it.

It's amazing how many very clever men and women get too bogged down in day to day headaches to see what is actually causing their difficulties. They assume that 'everything' is going wrong. Once the barrier has been pointed out to them they begin to realise that their problems can be traced back to a root cause and they are halfway to solving it. When the problem has been overcome, the success line is likely to continue it's journey.

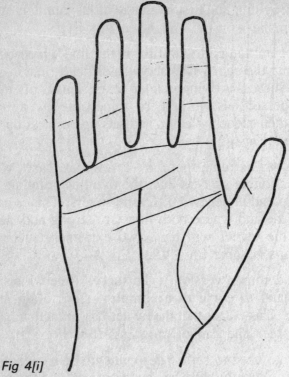

Fig 4[i]

George's story

Of all the larger lines on the hand I think the success line is the one which changes the most frequently. I remember a client called George who ran a successful wholesale business. His success line ran straight up his hand to end under the third finger of Apollo and there was also a star under the little finger of Mercury. Both very good signs, indicating success and money in his chosen career. (See Fig 4[j])

However, the next time I saw George it was obvious that something was wrong. There were stress lines all over his palm, particularly around the heartline and his success line was starting to fade. It turned out that

50

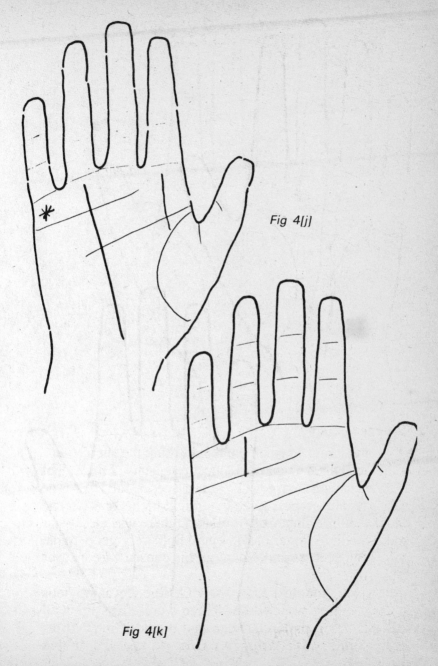

Fig 4[j]

Fig 4[k]

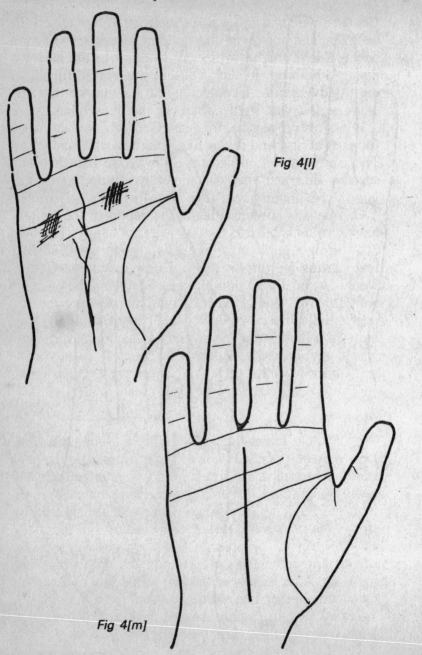

Fig 4[l]

Fig 4[m]

George's wife was miserable. She wanted him to sell the business and move to the country. George was torn between love for his wife and devotion to the business that he'd built up. In such a case it was very difficult for me to advise him. I could only stress that he must do what he felt was right, whatever the consequences.

It was over a year before I saw George again and when I looked at his hand it was like reading a different palm. The line of ambition had faded away, so had the main success line and the star under his little finger had vanished without trace. (See Fig 4[k])

George was now installed in the depths of the country having sold his business and he was not happy. The only comforting sign I could find was a new, small success line starting high in his hand. This showed that George would eventually go into business again and the business would thrive. Well, a year or two later George took an interest in landscape gardening and being George, he soon built up a modest business. He was happy and his wife was happy, but he never repeated his early success. The star under his little finger never returned.

Fiona's story

I saw another interesting success line at around this time. I can only describe it as a line which wiggled up the palm and then branched out in several different directions. The client was a smart, expensively dressed woman from the North of England, let's call her Fiona for the sake of this story. She ran several different businesses, all sucessful, as shown in the branching lines, but the wiggle in the success line intrigued me. I examined it with a magnifying glass. After each twist the line would start to straighten out, then another line would come in from the side and knock it off course again. Around the heartline there were little stress grilles. (See Fig 4[l])

I realised from this that the woman was having problems which were affecting her career and that the difficulties were associated with her private life since they clustered round the heartline. Her fingertips were soft, showing that she was a kind woman and found it painful to deal with her problems.

Afterwards I discovered that her marriage was in trouble and each fresh 'outrage' as she saw it, from her husband threw her into such turmoil that her career suffered. It was clear that for her own survival she was going to have to grit her teeth and tackle the marriage problems once and for all. She went away determined to do so. The last I heard she was getting a divorce and her success line was straight and clear. (See Fig 4[m])

CHAPTER FIVE:
WILL YOU MAKE A MILLION?

The young woman was neat but rather careworn. There were dark circles under her eyes and her hair was carefully brushed rather than expensively coiffeured. Her clothes were attractive but not exactly haute couture. She looked in fact rather like many of the people who find their way to my door. Neither rich nor poor but struggling with some sort of problem.

So I was quite surprised when I opened her hand and saw money written all over it. There was a star at the base of her hand on the outer side, a star under the first finger of Jupiter and under the little finger of Mercury there was a diamond, a very unusual shape indeed. All these marks together added up to an enormous amount of money and anyone finding such signs in their hand can expect a fortune.

Sally's story

Sally (I can't use her real name for legal reasons) wasn't rich yet however. The other lines on her hand showed that her life was in a tangle and it would take some time before she sorted out her complicated affairs and took possession of her millions. She had a clearly marked success line and just beside it was an inheritance line, a line which ran straight through the heart and headline and up to the third finger of Apollo. (See Fig 5[a])

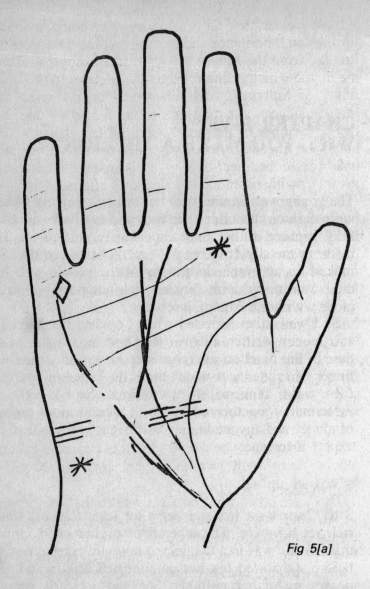

Fig 5[a]

It was clear that Sally's money was going to come through an inheritance and to confirm this, a very strong line ran from the Mount of Venus (the fleshy pad under the thumb which is encircled by the lifeline) to the small finger of Mercury. Any line which begins inside the lifeline suggests a strong link to the family or one particular member of the family and the fact that it ended under the finger of Mercury pointed towards a business link because the finger of Mercury is amongst other things involved with business and financial affairs.

Sally's money would come from some sort of family business I was sure. But it wasn't going to be easy to come by. Branching off the family line was another line which broke up messily at the end. The frayed end of the line indicated a discrepancy somewhere, connected to the family and the business but not involving a member of the family since the blemish was not actually on the family line but linked to it.

Afterwards Sally explained that her father had owned several mines and promised her that she would never want for anything. Sadly he died unexpectedly when she was still a child, someone else had taken over his business and somehow the fortune Sally had been promised never materialised. There were travel lines all over her hand and I realised that she would inherit her fortune eventually but there would be a lot of legal work and travelling before she did so.

There are other signs of great wealth that can be seen in the hand. Two parallel success lines running straight up the hand from the wrist and ending under the third finger of Apollo show riches on the way. The last person I saw with these lines became a millionaire not long afterwards. (See Fig 5[b])

Great success and financial gain also await the person with a single success line going straight to Apollo with

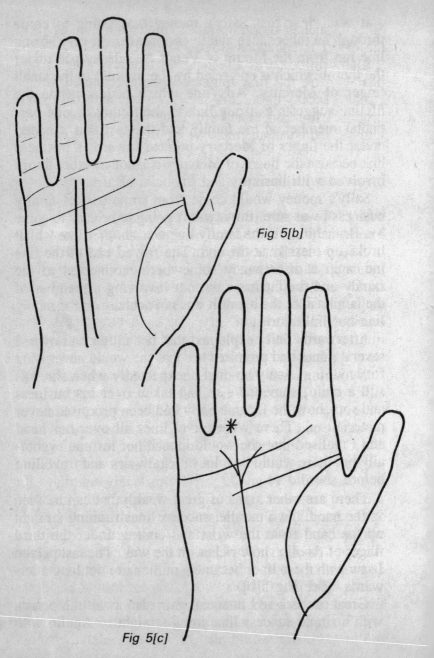

Fig 5[b]

Fig 5[c]

other branches shooting out. If there is a star as well, the effect is enhanced. (See Fig 5[c]).

Many millionaires also have particularly long second phalange on the first finger of Jupiter coupled with a strong success line. This shows an exceptionally good organiser in business and providing the subject works for himself and is not an employee, it usually leads to wealth.

Managing millions

The Duke of Westminster

The Duke of Westminster is reputedly the richest man in Britain. His hands are long and slim and surprisingly his fingers taper towards the tips which turn back. This shows that despite his logical mind he also has psychic abilities of which he might not be aware. The fingers of Apollo and Saturn are very long indicating that he can influence others when he wishes. He is also inclined to take a calculated risk in business.

Wealthy men are often believed to be mean but in the case of the Duke of Westminster I would say that he is quite a kind-hearted character because he has a full mount of Venus and the skin texture of his hands appears soft. There is a slight curve on the outside of his palm showing an appreciation of beautiful things and I would imagine he enjoys good food. He probably entertains for pleasure as well as business. Despite this amiable appearance, the Duke is not a soft touch. His fingertips are firm and his thumb is very determined. I feel that he wouldn't tolerate laziness in others and can be stubborn at times.

In a hand like this you would expect to find a success line that runs straight to Apollo with branches to Mercury and Jupiter — an indication of wealth running into millions. A star would also be shown under the finger

Jeffrey Archer (far right), Richard Branson (middle) and fitness club manager Julie Franchett participate in Motivation Week.

of Mercury and since the Duke has inherited his position there would be a line of inheritance cutting across the headline into the success line.

Richard Branson

Richard Branson is a self-made millionaire and this shows in the slope at the base of his fingers leading down to the small finger of Mercury. His hands are long and slim and the first three fingers are almost the same length. Branson is obviously a born leader with the ability to talk his way in and out of any situation. He is also a risk taker and so far this has paid off.

Despite his adventurous approach to business I imagine he would be quite careful with money since his mount of Venus begins shallow and broadens as it moves down the palm. This doesn't imply a miserly temperament, more an appreciation of the value of money. This particular mount of Venus belongs to someone who gets on well with others but is not over concerned with other people's opinions of him. The firm tips to his fingers indicate that he will not tolerate outside interference in his affairs.

Jeffrey Archer

Jeffrey Archer is the millionaire author of many best sellers. His creative talent shows in the curve at the side of his hand and the concentration required to sit for hours over a typewriter is reflected in his long, methodical fingers. He appears to be a kind man, since his mount of Venus is full, his heartline long and his fingers look soft. Nevertheless he can also be stubborn as his thumb is stiff.

He probably has strong intuitive powers because the tips of his fingers turn back slightly and there is a line of intuition visible on the edge of his palm. He is probably unaware of these gifts but draws heavily on them in his work without realising it. Archer's small finger of

Mercury is long indicating an articulate personality and judging by the length of his Apollo finger he probably takes risks now and then.

His fingers have square tips and his palm is square and I would say that despite his early misfortunes in business, Jeffrey Archer would make a good businessman.

Making money is not the same as becoming seriously rich. It's no good making a million one day and losing it the next. If the fingers are set wide apart it shows that money slips right through them and wealth can't be consolidated unless the subject makes a very determined effort to change his ways.

If the second finger of Saturn is short it shows a frivolous nature unlikely to use money wisely. If the third finger of Apollo is too long the gambling instinct may prove so strong that the owner will risk and lose his fortune and if the lifeline sweeps in too wide a curve round the base of the thumb creating a full, plump Mount of Venus, the person will be too generous to hang on to money for long. If the fingertips are soft as well they are likely to fall for hard luck stories and end up giving away a great deal.

The person who uses money wisely will have a Mount of Venus that is not too full, fairly firm fingertips and the heart and headline will be close together.

Running the Royal Family firm

The Queen
The Queen is the richest woman in Britain and looking at photographs of her hand, I can see that she is very good with money. If she hadn't been Queen she would have made a very good business woman.

She has the typical square business hand, emphasised by capable square finger tips and even phalanges. She

The Queen presenting the Queen's Cup polo trophy to the Marquess
of Milford Haven
© *Topham Picture Library*

is very determined as shown by her stiff thumb — an asset
in business though she could be inclined to stubbornness
at times. Her fingertips are firm showing that she doesn't
like to be told what to do and her first finger of Jupiter
leans slightly towards the second finger of Saturn revealing that once she's made up her mind about something
she won't budge an inch.

The first finger of Jupiter is long showing leadership
qualities and her small finger of Mercury leans out from
the other fingers — this means that she can stand up and
speak well in front of others.

The mount of Venus widens gradually as it curves
round the palm showing that she is not mean but neither
is she reckless with money. She is also very shrewd, as
proved by her knotty joints and narrow palm.

Privately the Queen is kind and thoughtful — the mount of Venus being wide and she has a grand sense of humour — shown by the wide gap between her head and heartlines. She has to guard against depression now and then I would say because her headline slopes rather steeply and she could be possessive at times because her heartline rises up towards the fingers.

She does not appear to be artistic — there is no curve to the side of the hand but the soft texture of her skin shows a love of beautiful things. Between the thumb and the first finger of Jupiter on the outer side, the full web of soft flesh reveals a love of animals. Had she not been Queen I think her Majesty would have done very well in some business involving horses.

Prince Charles

Prince Charles has a wide, knotty hand revealing him to be shrewd but thoughtful. He has compassion for people less fortunate than himself. The width of his hand also shows a sensuous nature.

The fingers are long revealing a methodical mind and the firm texture of his skin shows a fondness for outdoor pursuits. He's got a very long thumb showing an intellectual nature and since the tip of the thumb is conic in shape he has a psychic ability. The first joint is curved denoting tact and flexibility but the second joint is long signifying a very strong will.

His heartline runs straight across his palm showing that he is not possessive. His headline is very long, I would say that he has a wonderful memory.

The outer side of his palm is slightly curved showing an appreciation of the arts. He is probably a very lovable character because the curve of Venus is very full. This also shows that he is likely to be generous with money.

Like his mother, Prince Charles is a very private person since he holds his hands close to his body. In fact most

Prince Charles on a visit to London's East End
© *Topham Picture Library*

of the Royal Family seem to hide their hands whenever possible.

Prince Charles' love of people would in other circumstances have suited him to a career in social work psychology or even healing.

Prince Philip

Prince Philip would have made a natural businessman. He has square hands, and long square fingers showing a capable mind and attention to detail. His hands appear to be wide revealing a sensuous nature and he has a curve at the side of his palm suggesting artistic talent.

He has a wonderful sense of humour shown by the wide gap between his head and heartlines and he is a natural

65

leader, having a long first finger of Jupiter. There are times when he is probably moody because his headline slopes fairly steeply and since his hands are firm rather than flexible he is inclined to be domineering.

Finally it might be an old cliche that money doesn't bring happiness, but it's surprising how often signs of wealth in the hands are accompanied by downward sloping lines falling away from the heartline which show disappointments and unhappiness in love. Frequently the headline drops steeply towards the wrist as well, suggesting depression and loneliness. I suppose it's true that you can't have everything.

CHAPTER SIX:
THE HAND THAT MEANS BUSINESS

To be successful in business you need to be shrewd with an instinctive grasp of what will work and what will not. Intellect, drive and a healthy success line can be wasted if they are applied in a field which simply doesn't suit you. Some people for instance would be better off using their talents in politics or the arts or some other area where their valuable gifts can be put to the best possible use. Success and wealth can be found in many different walks of life.

The natural businessman usually has a square palm, a well developed first finger of Jupiter, and head and heart lines which are straight and strongly marked. His finger-tips would be square or rounded, his hand springy in texture and both phalanges of the thumb would be strong and even.

A three-pronged fork at the end of the heart line pointing towards Jupiter shows great business acumen. So do three lines running up from the life line, crossing the head line and continuing on up to the first finger.

Perhaps most important of all are the knotty joints to the fingers – a sign of great shrewdness.

But I realise, looking back, that I have been talking about 'the natural businessman', yet women are just as likely to possess that magical flair as men and increasingly they are using it with great success.

Thirty years ago, when I first began studying palms

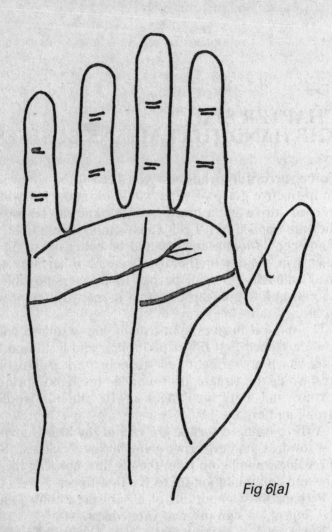

Fig 6[a]

seriously, my male clients tended to come to me with business worries while my female clients were more interested in romance and the number of children they might bear.

These days it's very different. Now the men are just as interested in relationships as the women – or perhaps it's just that they are less shy of admitting it – and the women are just as likely to ask about their careers as about matters of the heart.

Every year the number of businesswomen coming through my door seems to increase and I have been looking at their palms with particular interest. At first glance you might assume their hands were quite different from those of their male colleagues. I'm usually confronted by a smaller, more feminine hand with long, elegantly polished nails, the fingers adorned with rings and occasionally even the wrists decorated by bracelets or attractive fashion watches. Yes, at first, there appears to be no similarity to the male business hand at all.

Yet when you look closer, and ignore all these superficial, feminine trappings, it's surprising how alike the male and female business hands really are. Beneath those perfectly manicured oval nails Ms Businesswoman has square, practical fingertips, a square palm and a strong, long finger of Jupiter, just like her male counterpart. Like him she will probably also have the three-pronged fork at the end of the heart line revealing her instinctive business acumen.

But despite all this the male and female business hands are not interchangeable in everything but size. There are important differences and I've come to the conclusion that these occur because although we're supposed to live in a land of equal opportunities, women still have a tougher time reaching the top in business than men. Both the struggles and the extra qualities needed to overcome them can be read in the typical businesswoman's palm.

Most obvious is the wide gap clearly seen between the start of the life line, high up in the palm and the start of the head line. This shows tremendous independence. As a child the future businesswoman might well have been a rebel or difficult for her parents to control because of her deep need to do things for herself.

In addition her fingertips are very firm proving that she hates to be told what to do and her thumb tends to be stiff and unyielding when bent gently away from the hand. This indicates a stubborn nature.

Now these qualities may not sound particularly flattering but for a woman in a tough business world they are probably essential. Stubbornness of course can be dangerous if it is extreme but a woman in business needs a certain obstinate streak to help her overcome the inevitable knocks she is going to face.

Interestingly these knocks also show up on the success line. The businessman often has a success line which runs straight to the finger of Apollo but most businesswomen I've seen tend to bear success lines which sweep up to the second finger of Saturn. This is a sign of hard work and struggle. Success will come but only as a result of the woman's own substantial efforts.

The last striking difference between the male and female business hand is in the length of the woman's small finger of Mercury. Generally the successful businesswoman will have an unusually long Mercury finger, reaching high above the third phalange of the Apollo finger next to it. This is the sign of an individual with a charming and persuasive tongue and when it is accomplished by a full Mount of Venus it suggests great tact as well.

Such Mercury fingers can also be found on businessmen but they are more common amongst women and I think this must indicate that businesswomen have learnt to get what they want by skillful manipulation of the people around them rather than by sheer force of personality.

Yet for all these similarities in their hands I don't wish to imply that every businesswoman is the same. So far I've mentioned the general outlines. The full character is revealed on closer examination. The personalities of individual businesswomen are as varied as their male counterparts. This was illustrated to me vividly recently when I met two businesswomen who couldn't have been more different.

Janis' Story

Janis was tall, well-dressed and brisk. I was slightly puzzled when I first met her because she did not seem to have any particular problem that she wanted to discuss but in the end I came to the conclusion that she was curious. She wanted to check me out in case she might need me in the future.

Although she was wearing smart, feminine clothes Janis' hands were surprisingly heavy. She had strikingly square palms and long but powerful square-tipped fingers. Her thumb was particularly heavy showing a bad temper. This was a woman you crossed at your peril.

The thumb was stiff too, indicating stubbornness, and while her head line stretched almost right across her palm in a straight line, her heart line was short and poorly developed. Combined with a narrow Mount of Venus formed by the life line clinging close to the base of the thumb instead of curving out into the palm this told me that Janis was a cool, unemotional, rather selfish character who preferred money and business to domestic life.

Janis was one of the few businesswomen who did not have a long Mercury finger but looking at that weighty thumb I realised she didn't need it. Janis probably got what she wanted because people were too frightened of her temper to disagree with her. She never had to resort to charm and persuasion.

I realised that I was dealing with a successful and efficient businesswoman here but I was very glad I didn't work for her.

It turned out that Janis ran a thriving truck company and there had been times when she was building the business when she went out and drove the trucks her sometimes driving all night and then returning 71 office to do the paperwork during the day.

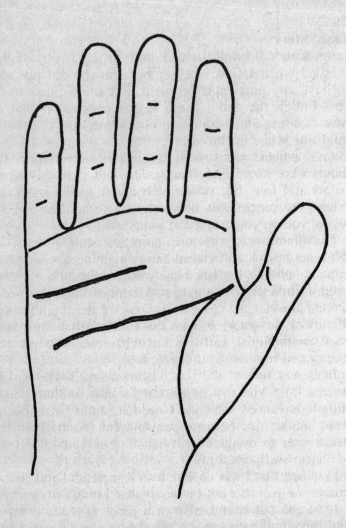

Janis' hand

She was a tough, hard-working lady, no doubt about it who deserved all the success that now came her way. There was just one thing. Did she, I wondered, ever think about relationships? Did she hope to get married one day?

Janis laughed out loud.

'Married?' she said, 'What for? I can get everything want for myself. I don't need a man.'

Elaine's Story

Elaine ran a small hairdressing business with her husband Paul. She was a small, neatly made woman wearing a casual flowing blouse tucked into beautifully fitting jeans.

She looked more like an artist than a businesswoman and when I saw the creative curve that swung from her wrist to the base of her small finger I would have sworn that she was a painter or poet. Yet when I turned her hand over I realised there was much more to Elaine than that.

She was artistic and creative of course but she also had a square, practical palm, square-tipped fingers, a three-pronged fork at the end of her heart line and a long Mercury finger.

Paul was very lucky to have such a partner. Elaine was a rare combination of artistic talent, business acumen and a wonderful communicator. While her nimble fingers performed their magic with her clients' hair, Elaine's easy charm won their loyalty and her clever business brain spotted the best possible use to which to put these assets.

Interestingly Elaine's success line ran straight to her third finger of Apollo showing that success had not been a struggle for her. I think it must have been the combination of her enormous charm and the fact that she was in partnership with her husband which allowed her to leap-frog the difficulties lone women so often face in business.

At any rate the only worry the couple shared was what to do next. Their salon happened to occupy a good position in a developing area and they'd been offered a substantial sum for the site. They were tempted to accept but

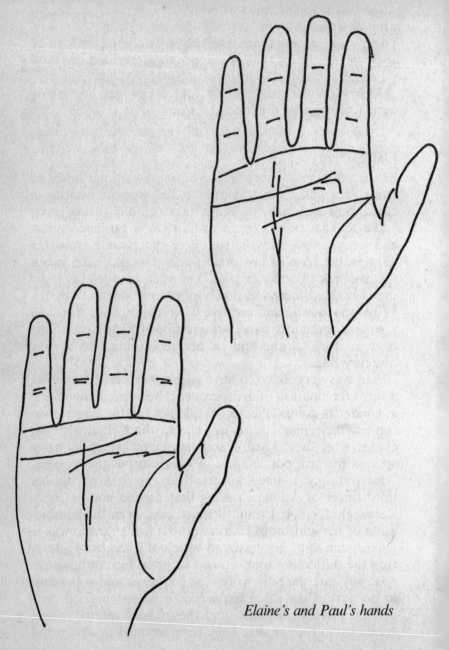

Elaine's and Paul's hands

something held them back. Did I think they were doing the right thing?

When I looked closely at Elaine's success line I noticed there was a series of breaks in it, indicating changes, but that after the breaks the line went straight on as before.

Paul's success line showed a similar pattern.

I interpreted this to mean that although there were changes coming they should still run the business much as before, but changed in some way. Could they diversify perhaps?

Elaine and Paul went away to think about it. Some time later I heard that soon after our meeting a different, unexpected change occurred. The shop next door to theirs suddenly became vacant and far from selling their own premises they bought the adjoining shop.

Now in addition to the hairdressing salon they run a sauna and beauty parlour and it's doing so well they are looking to expand further.

Unlike Janis, Elaine who had a wide Mount of Venus, was quite happy to share her life and her success with a partner. Both women had achieved what they wanted to achieve in their very different ways.

Anita Roddick

One of Britain's best known and most successful businesswomen today is Anita Roddick, founder of The Body Shop chain of cosmetic stores. From humble beginnings these distinctive shops have spread across the world and the products are now widely imitated – annoying perhaps for Ms Roddick but then as they say imitation is the sincerest form of flattery. It is a measure of the concept's success that so many companies want to copy it.

Ms Roddick has had her critics in recent years but then this too is a measure of success. If she was still struggling quietly with one small back street store the critics would not have noticed her but then neither

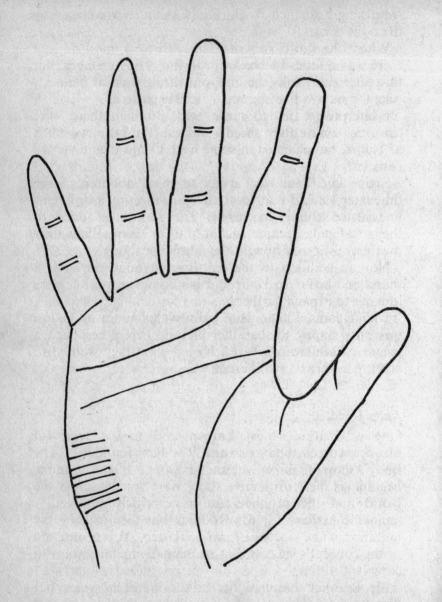

Anita Roddick's hand

would anyone else. Fortunately, a glance at Ms Roddick's hands assured me that she is tough enough to ride out the storms.

These hands are firm and capable, rather long with a distinct square appearance from the wrist to the base of the fingers. The square palm is indicative of a practical nature while the long fingers reveal a love of detail – two qualities which don't often go together.

This hand is feminine but it is also strong and shrewd. The finger joints are knotty and the tips are square which shows that this lady has acute judgment and cannot easily be deceived.

The thumb is rather stiff and large hinting at a stubborn streak and the headlines vary. In one hand the headline is straight while the other has a gentle slope. Once again this is an unusual combination. The straight headline shows a practical, businesslike approach while the sloping line indicates imagination and flair. Put these two qualities together and you have a person who can produce something creative and new in a businesslike way – a rare talent indeed!

What's more this is someone who has never liked to follow the crowd. The headline is separate from the lifeline revealing an independent nature and the fingertips are hard, the sign of a person who doesn't like to follow orders. These characteristics are found in people who are perfectly suited to being self-employed. I believe that fairly early in life Ms Roddick found the career path that was tailor made for her and wisely she stuck to it.

The outer side of the palm is scored with many horizontal lines pointing in towards the centre of the hand – a certain sign of frequent travel and the success line shows up in several positions, sometimes an indication of many different careers but in this case I would say it mirrors the diversity of Ms Roddick's beauty products.

All in all this is an unusual hand. Creative yet practical, talented but shrewd, stubborn yet charming. A pretty good recipe for success.

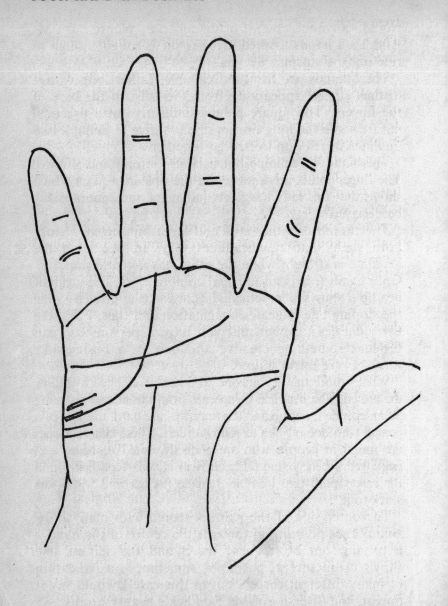

Irene Stein's hand

Irene Stein

This is a very interesting hand. Irene Stein I believe launched an amazingly successful new health product, Regina Royal Jelly, at a time when very few people outside the dedicated health food fraternity had ever heard of the substance. Within months it seemed, Royal Jelly was being hailed as a wonder food and now we find it in every supermarket and chemist shop alongside the vitamin supplements and cold remedies. It is so common today we take it for granted and for this, in large part we have to thank Irene.

Like Anita Roddick, Irene Stein's hands are long and feminine and she possesses those shrewd, knotty finger joints without which any person entering business would be at a sad disadvantage.

Her long fingers suggest that she is careful over details and leaves nothing to chance, while her strong, firm thumb reveals her staying power. Once she has come to a decision she will stick with it through thick and thin if necessary.

The combination of these qualities, though rare in general are often found in the hands of successful business people. What is strikingly different about Ms Stein's hand is her success line.

Most success lines, if they exist at all, run straight up the hand showing a clear-cut goal achieved fairly easily, or they may be broken in several pieces indicating a number of different careers or false starts. In Ms Stein's case her success line ran straight to the headline and stopped dead. But then another success line rose from the travel line and shot steeply up to the third finger of Apollo – a wonderful place for a success line to end, indicating a venture that brings wealth and good luck.

It seemed as if Ms Stein had been following a career which led nowhere until one day, on a foreign trip she found the correct path to be travelling.

I was interested to learn the almost legendary story since told about the introduction of Regina Royal Jelly.

Apparently Ms Stein was leading a fairly unspectacular life until she made a journey to Greece. There she fell into conversation with a very old man who had kept bees and as they chatted he told her about a wonderful substance known as Royal Jelly because it was fed to Queen Bees.

Ms Stein was intrigued by the properties attributed to this rarefied form of honey. She tried it herself and was so impressed, she decided to market it.

Whether this story has been embroidered in the telling I don't know. All I can say is that it ties in perfectly with the marks on Irene Stein's hand.

CHAPTER SEVEN:
ARE YOU GOOD AT DECISION MAKING?

It's always sad when you meet someone with talent who has failed to fulfil their potential. Particularly when their progress has been blighted by a flaw which ought to be easy to put right and yet it seems impossible for them to do so. I met just such a man a couple of years ago. To spare his embarrassment I'll call him Philip. Philip was a very clever man, he worked in computers and he'd invented some new system which ought to have guaranteed a meteoric rise in his career. There was a rise all right but it didn't happen to Philip. It was his boss who ended up with all the glory. Philip remained in the back room overlooked by everyone.

Philip's story

His hand told the whole story. There were many good, positive aspects in Philip's palm but they were all held in abeyance by the unfortunate merging of his head and lifelines. (See Fig 7[a]) The headline was joined to his lifeline and did not separate until the middle of his palm. This showed that Philip couldn't make a decision. He couldn't even make up his mind to leave the company, or to tackle his exploitive boss. He was still tied to his family who had been telling him what to do for so long that he couldn't now make up his mind about anything.

Reinforcing this pattern was a line running from the

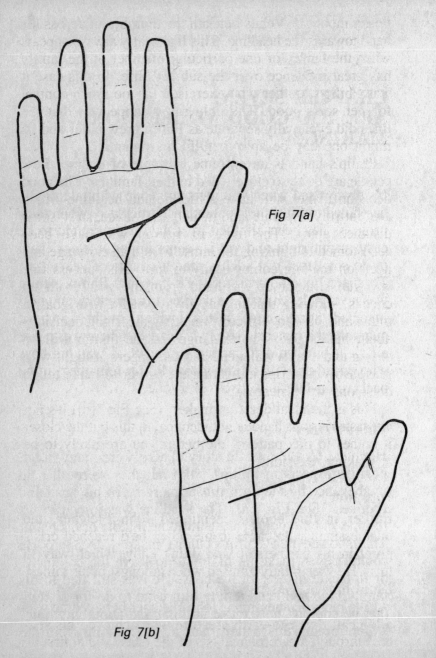

Fig 7[a]

Fig 7[b]

fleshy mount of Venus beneath the thumb, out across his hand towards the headline. This line nearly always appears when the family or one particular member of the family has great influence over the subject's life. In this case it was Philip's mother who exercised far too much control for her son's good. The only ray of hope was that the lines did eventually separate as Philip grew older and he might one day be able to fulfil his potential.

Philip's hand is an extreme example of course. Few people are quite so closely tied to their families. The good decision maker will have a lifeline and headline which are entirely separate and which may even start some distance apart. This type of person will have been accustomed to thinking for himself from an early age and decision making comes easily to him. His success line will run straight up the hand from the wrist with no checks, showing that he has always had a firm goal in mind and has no difficulty making the right decisions about his career. The phalanges of the thumb will be strong and evenly balanced and the fingers straight with reasonably firm tips indicating the power to make tough decisions when necessary.

This is the ideal decision-maker. (See Fig 7[b]) It's not a disaster if your hand is not identical to this but the closer it comes to this pattern, the better you are likely to be at making decisions.

Intuition

Earlier in this book I mentioned John Fletcher, the businessman who came to me when he'd reached crisis point in his partnership and didn't know which way to turn. He was greatly amused when amongst other things, I told him he was psychic.

Like most businessmen, John Fletcher believed he was a logical, down-to-earth creature who achieved his success through a careful analysis of the facts, and at first he was inclined to dismiss the idea that his decisions could be based on 'mere' intuition.

This is a very common reaction. I suppose businessmen associate psychic powers with crystal balls, darkened rooms and a penchant for very large hoop ear-rings. Yet everybody is psychic to a certain degree — only they don't call it psychic — they say they are intuitive. And some people are more intuitive than others.

Businessmen (not realising they are talking about the same thing) tend to be just as dismissive of intuition as they are of psychic power. Intuition, many believe, is all right for superstitious old women but it has no place in the sophisticated modern world of business. I've never been able to understand this reasoning. Why should logic and intuition be mutually exclusive? Surely if you could add intuition to a logical mind you would have the best of both worlds?

The sceptical businessman may scoff at the very idea. But I've got news for him. He may not know it but he is using his psychic power, his intuition, every day of the week. I don't suppose there is a successful business-man in the world who lacks the gift of intuition. I'd go further and say that the men and women at the very top of every tree, the ones whose careers have been the most spectacular, are probably the most psychic of the lot.

Such people get 'gut feelings', they follow their 'hunches' and like John Fletcher, they wake up some mornings **'just knowing'** that it's the right time to sell. They are using a very valuable gift in the decision-making process. The gift of intuition and I think this gift has to be added to the list of qualities essential to the businessman.

Intuition, like most other things, can be seen in the hand. There is actually a line of intuition. It begins under the little finger of Mercury and curves down the hand in a semi-circle to rest at the base of the palm on the out-side edge. (See Fig 7[c]) If there is no line visible it doesn't

84

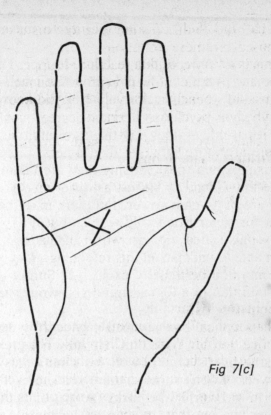

Fig 7[c]

mean you lack intuition. It is more likely that you haven't learned to use it yet. Some people use their intuition instinctively, others tend to ignore those inner promptings because they don't understand them. Yet the more you use intuition the more the gift develops.

There are a few rare people who also have a large, clearly marked cross between their headline and heartline. This is called the Mystic Cross and shows a very high degree of psychic power. These people could take up psychic work if they chose to develop their gift. If not, they will still use it unconsciously in whatever career they choose to follow. They will be known for their remarkable foresight and their uncanny ability to make the right decision.

I explained most of this to John Fletcher. I don't think he was convinced, but he did admit that much of his success was due to his peculiar talent of 'just knowing' when the time was right to sell shares.

'That's psychic power,' I said.
'Instinct,' said John.

Well as far as I'm concerned, a rose by any other name. . . !

Running the country

Sir Winston Churchill

Some time ago I was fortunate enough to see a model of the hand of Sir Winston Churchill. The great man had died some years before, but nevertheless it was fascinating to see the likeness of his hand perfect in every detail — even to the ring that he always wore on his third finger.

Churchill's hands were wide and the outside of the palm was curved showing a great love of art so I am not surprised to read of his many painting expeditions. His first finger of Jupiter was long revealing leadership abilities that became obvious during World War Two. The second finger of Saturn was also very long and strong and this combined with a dominant first phalange on the thumb gave him the power to impose his will on others.

The heartline was very strong — long and deeply marked meaning that he was a compassionate man. This also shows in the softness of the palm and fingers. In his private life he was probably very considerate, particularly since the mount of Venus was very full showing a lovable nature. the headline sloped gently downwards and ended in a writers' fork. This indicated a strong imagination, love of art and, of course a writing ability.

The success line started at the base of his palm and broke in several places indicating changes in his career. The line ended under the third finger of Apollo showing that he was successful in everything he pursued.

In the centre of the palm he had a triangle adjoined to his success line suggesting honours in his early years. The small finger of Mercury was unusually long showing that he was a good communicator – and as we all know his oratory powers were legendary. He was also a wonderful writer.

One glance at this strong, powerful hand is enough to show that this man was destined for greatness.

John Major

John Major has flexible palms surmounted by medium fingers and the texture of his skin is dry. This shows that he listens to the opinions of others but is inclined to change his mind frequently.

Interestingly his first finger of Jupiter is longer than average but not as long as that of the typical 'born' leader, so I would say that, although he wants to lead, it doesn't come easily, or naturally to him.

He has a long small finger of Mercury showing that persuasion and diplomacy are his forte. He's a good talker behind the scenes but since his first finger of Jupiter is not dominant he finds it difficult to transfer his gift with words to the public arena. Public speaking has to be worked at. He's not a natural orator.

The Mount of Venus behind the life line begins thin and then gradually becomes fuller as it moves down the hand. This shows a character who is shrewd with money and who will think carefully before spending. He's not grasping but he's definitely not extravagant.

The fullness of the Mount of Venus at the bottom of the hand reveals a love of family and this coupled with the soft pads of the fingertips suggests a man who is fundamentally soft-hearted. He doesn't like to hurt people and will say what they wish to hear in order to avoid offending them.

Despite this he is a stickler for law and order and obeying the rules as shown by the fairly long, straight head line. This man insists on things being done properly.

I would say that John Major enjoys being Prime Minister but it's a difficult job for him and since he is a natural worrier, his palms are covered with tiny criss-cross lines. Despite the cool exterior, he lives on his nerves.

Tony Blair

Some time ago when Tony Blair first came to the forefront of his party his youthful appearance and wide eyes earned him the nickname Bambi. But anyone who assumes that the Labour leader is some sort of docile pet is in for a shock. One look at his hands reveals a very different character.

Tony Blair's hands are long and very slim, indicative of a strong-willed personality. His thumb is also long showing drive and it tapers slightly at the joint revealing a very shrewd and determined nature. He could even be stubborn at times but since his first and second fingers are almost the same length he can put his views across easily and probably wins people over to his opinion without too much argument.

His fingers are knotty, reinforcing the shrewdness of his mind but the tips are rounded indicating a methodical approach. He has a wonderful sense of humour because the gap between his head line and heart line is wide but although he appears easy to get along with he's not as soft as he seems. His fingertips are firm, revealing a person who will not tolerate anyone telling him what to do. Even if they are members of his own family.

President Clinton

President Clinton's hands are very interesting. Deeply pink and large with broad based fingers they show a sensuous, versatile and placid nature. He has a marked curve on the outer edge of the palm revealing creative talent and this so strong that I feel if he hadn't gone into politics this man could have been an entertainer of some kind.

He has a dominant first finger of Jupiter as well as a strong small finger of Mercury showing that he is a natural communicator and in his element in front of an audience. This gift is especially important for an American president who has to do well on radio and TV.

Interestingly, like President Reagan before him, Clinton has a slightly waisted thumb indicating a need for support in his efforts and looking at the hands of his wife Hillary, I can see that he has chosen the perfect partner to provide it.

Mrs Clinton has strong, square hands and her fingers of Jupiter and Mercury are almost the same length showing that she is a pretty good communicator herself. Her joints are knotty indicating a shrewd brain and her fingers tilt back slightly revealing an intuitive streak. This is a woman who gets instincts about people – liking or disliking them on sight and events usually prove her right.

She is an excellent rock for her husband to lean on.

CHAPTER EIGHT:
HAVE YOU GOT
THE KILLER INSTINCT?

There is a lot of talk about the killer instinct in business. The successful businessman is supposed to be tough and ruthless, able to go for the jugular when necessary without suffering a twinge of remorse. No doubt in a lot of businesses this quality is indispensable. After all it wouldn't be much good for health or efficiency if the businessman or woman lay awake night after night tortured by guilt every time they had to make a tough decision.

Nevertheless there is something rather unattractive about the sort of person who can cold-bloodedly decimate other businesses and careers without a pang and I believe that the killer instinct isn't always essential. I have known many successful people who have managed perfectly well without it. Often, charm, persuasiveness and a quick brain can work wonders where a ruthless approach would fail.

On the other hand, it has to be said that the rare creature, a ruthless person who also has great charm and tremendous powers of persuasion, would be quite devastating. Perhaps it's just as well that you don't often find these qualities combined.

● Ruthlessness

Sometimes difficult decisions have to be made. Staff have to be fired, other companies taken over, rival businesses beaten into submission. An oversensitive person might procrastinate endlessly to the detriment of the firm over such decisions while a tougher type would act without pain.

The ruthless man will have a strong thumb with a well developed first phalange. His hands will be hard and unyielding to the touch. Since such a person cares little for the feelings of others, selfishness will show in the shallow curve of the lifeline as it works round the base of the thumb and also in the waisted second joint of the thumb.

The headline is likely to be straight and unsloping and if the heartline and the headline are close together this person will also be very careful in financial matters. (See Fig 8[a])

● **Charm**

Charm comes in useful in every walk of life and business is no exception. There are people you warm to instantly and others who just can't seem to project a personality at all. Charm is not necessarily accompanied by any genuinely nice characteristics, but nevertheless it smooths the possessors path through life.

The charmer usually has a slim hand with short fingers, a very strong heartline and a success line that goes up towards the second finger of Saturn with a branch line veering towards Jupiter. If the sweep of the lifeline is very wide and full as well, this person would be irresistible. (See Fig 8[b])

● **Persuasiveness**

We've all met people who could sell sand in the Sahara and persuade you that day is night if they wish. Such types are extremely useful in business because there are very few professions that don't involve selling in some form.

Natural persuaders have a flexible thumb, soft skin, soft

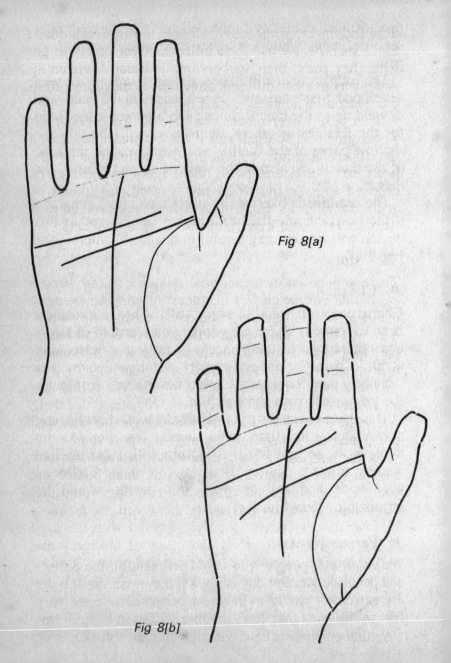

Fig 8[a]

Fig 8[b]

flesh and fingertips that curve slightly towards each other. Since such people use their influence over others to get what they want, their success line is usually broken up and points in many different directions as they move from one person to another. (See Fig 8[c])

Such power over others can be used for good or ill. These gifts will be used well if the persuader has a well developed heartline and a good headline but if the heartline is thin and poor, the fingers inclined to be crooked and the thumb deeply waisted, he should be avoided at all costs. He is likely to be devious and untrustworthy. He could even turn out to be a conman.

Vic's story

The combination of these three qualities in one person is unusual but the closest I came to meeting an example of it was when I read the palm of a wealthy cafe owner. Vic, as I'll call him, was a little short of natural charm perhaps but he more than made up for it with his smooth tongue and carefully concealed ruthlessness.

One summer, returning from holiday Vic pulled into an all-night cafe for a cup of coffee. He noticed that there was quite a bit of land around the place and it was well positioned on a busy holiday and transport route.

At that hour the cafe was almost deserted and Vic took care to fall into conversation with the man behind the counter. By his second coffee Vic had discovered that this man was the owner and he'd been in the business for over twenty years. Vic sympathised with the long hours, the ceaseless work, the years of drudgery and before long he'd convinced the man that he was tired of the whole thing and would be glad of a change. By the time he left, Vic had secured a promise that if the owner should think of selling he would offer him first refusal. 'I'll look in next week when you've had time to think it over,' said Vic as he left.

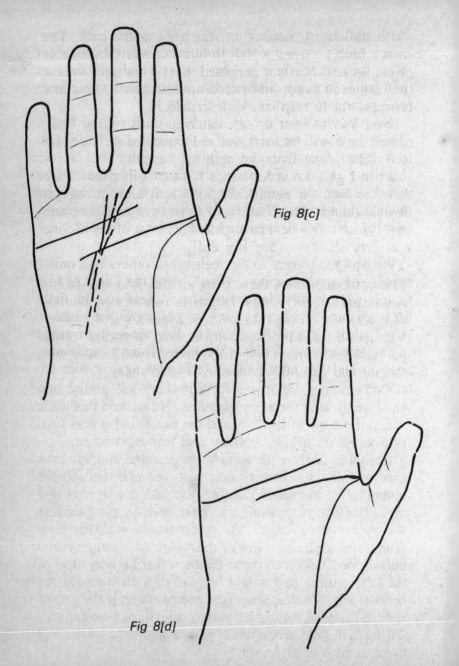

Fig 8[c]

Fig 8[d]

The following Sunday he was back at the cafe. The owner finally agreed to sell to him at a very reasonable price. Secretly Vic was delighted, but he managed to beat the man even lower and ended up with house, land and business for 'a snip' as he described it.

Soon Vic had put up self catering units on the land, turned the house into an hotel and expanded the cafe. He looks like going from strength to strength.

When I glanced at his hands I wasn't surprised to see that Vic had the persuaders soft flesh and strong yet flexible thumb. His headline was straight and long and fairly close to his heartline while the curve of his lifeline was very shallow. (See Fig 8[d])

Vic was indifferent to the feelings of others and quite capable of ruthless action. What's more the joints of his fingers were knotty, indicating shrewdness and his first finger of Jupiter was very long suggesting either leadership qualities in a positive hand or a domineering nature in a negative hand. Vic had the killer instinct, no doubt about it and I wouldn't like to come up against him in business.

CHAPTER NINE:
ASSESSING YOUR JOB POTENTIAL

It's surprising how many people end up in the wrong career. Despite career advice at school and talks from various experts, thousands of young people still take jobs for which they are unsuited. I expect the situation is getting even worse now that unemployment is relatively high. People are prepared to take any work offered to them rather than sit at home watching their confidence ebb away.

There's nothing wrong with that attitude, of course, but unfortunately a lot of people get stuck in the wrong field far too long. Such a false start can waste valuable time which would be better spent gaining experience in the right area.

Pamela's story

Pamela Southgate, a former client who has since become a friend was just such a case. When I first met Pamela she was discontented with her life in general but couldn't pin down exactly what was wrong. She didn't tell me this at first of course. It was all there in her hand. In the centre of her palm was a faint spider's web of curving lines — a sign of dissatisfaction and beside it was a line that stretched from the outside of her hand up towards the first finger of Jupiter. This line was in fact an ambition line but way off course, showing that the ambition had not been achieved. Incidentally, 'off-course' lines are very difficult for beginners to spot. They can only be recognised with practise. There was no sign of a success line. (See Fig 9[a])

Yet Pamela was a very talented lady. The outside edge of her hand had a deep curve showing that she was artistic and creative. I gathered from this that Pamela's frustration was connected with unfulfilled ambitions and that these ambitions were probably something to do with an artistic career.

Pamela was amazed. It turned out that she loved painting and drawing. In fact as a teenager she was considered so promising that she was sent to art college. But somehow, surrounded by so many clever and talented people Pamela's confidence drained away and she didn't think she was good enough to consider a career in art.

Instead she took a job in a reference library. It was a very good job. Pamela was secure and well paid. Many people would have been glad to change places with her. Yet good as she was at her library work, Pamela was not fulfilling her potential. She had spent 30 years in the wrong job. I suggested she approach some publishers with her drawings and ask for an opinion. Pamela did so and not long afterwards she was commissioned to illustrate a children's book.

Since then more commissions have been coming in and soon she will have to choose whether to become a full-time illustrator. A success line has now appeared on Pamela's hand, the dissatisfaction web has gone and the line of ambition is back in it's proper place. Pamela will do very well, of that I have no doubt, but what a pity she had to wait so long to find out where her true talents lay. (See Fig 9[b])

Shaping up

To assess your abilities you need to go back to the basic

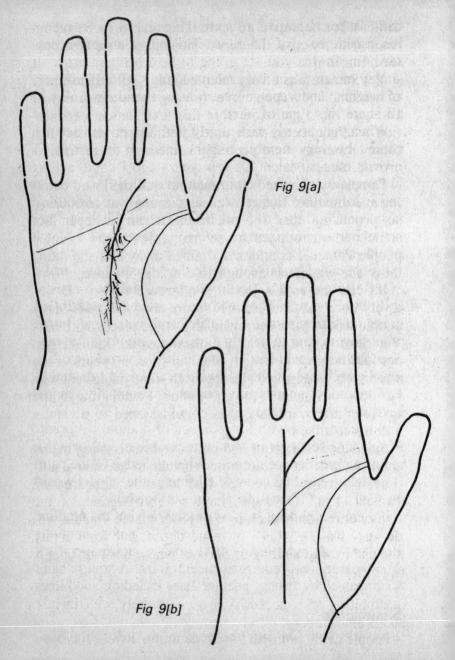

Fig 9[a]

Fig 9[b]

hand shapes. Creative gifts are indicated by the curve on the outside edge of the palm. This curve doesn't necessarily mean that you are going to be a brilliant artist. It simply means talent in a creative area. A gifted designer, an original landscape gardener, an outstanding cook will all share this type of hand.

When the curve is particularly pronounced and accompanied by very flexible fingers and soft fingertips, it reveals musical talent. A few years ago I came across just such a hand. The young man was called Barrie Stolla and it turned out that as well as playing just about any instrument you care to name he also wrote music. In fact it was Barrie who composed the TV theme tune for Match of the Day.

People with a creative curve to their hands should make every effort to find a career which will use their artistic abilities to the full. They will feel wasted and unfulfilled in any other occupation. Spatulate hands with large, broad blunt fingers tend to belong to people who prefer an outdoor life and would hate to be confined in a routine office job. Farmers, sportsmen, travellers and active businessmen who dash about from company to company tend to have this sort of hand.

A square hand with a square palm is quite different. People with this type of hand are capable of indoor work requiring great concentration. When the edge of the palm is straight, revealing no artistic leanings the subject would do well in law, accountancy or administration.

If there is no line of success or ambition but the headline is long, the owner of such a hand is a conscientious plodder — an asset in the civil service, academic work or any career that requires concentration. A square hand accompanied by strong, positive lines including good lines of ambition and success will do extremely well in just about any career.

People with pointed hands denoting love of beauty

99

should consider careers which bring them into contact with the lovely things they crave. Work in an art gallery, museum, the jewellery trade or antiques for example might well prove particularly satisfying. While those with conical hands would be very good in any career involving the public; social work, public relations and so on.

In most cases it is only possible to suggest the type of work which would suit the individual rather than a particular job, but there are one or two exceptions.

Occasionally I have seen a headline which ends in a distinct fork. (See Fig 9 [c]) This is known as the writer's fork and indicates literary talent. People with this type of headline should definitely try writing, even if they've never considered it before. They are likely to be surprised at their ability.

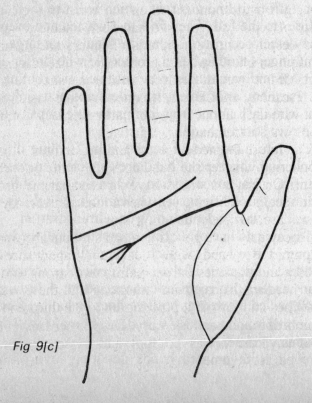

Fig 9[c]

If the owner of such a fork has a straight edge to his palm he is likely to be more successful writing on factual subjects, while a curve to the edge of the hand shows a budding novelist.

Other unusual hands tend to have stars strewn about the bottom of the palm. This is a sign of success in any career involving money. Banking, accountancy, the money market, would be ideal.

Good manual workers can be spotted by their low set thumb. This doesn't necessarily mean a lack of intelligence, simply that the subject is not ambitious in the material sense and would be happier in a job without responsibilities.

Tracey's story

Tracey was despondent when she came to see me. Like a lot of school leavers she had been unable to get a job and despite writing hundreds of letters she hadn't even secured an interview. Her problem was that academic subjects didn't interest her very much and she'd left school with scarcely a GCE to her name. Too late she discovered that in today's competitive job market her lack of qualifications was a tremendous drawback.

The future seemed hopeless and she arrived at my door wondering whether she was doomed to a life of unemployment. On paper I would have agreed that the prospects didn't seem too bright, yet when I looked at Tracey's hand I saw a completely different story.

Tracey may have got off to a bad start but she was going to go far. Her hands were square, the fingers shrewd and knotty and the lines on her palm were strong and clear. Her headline in particular was long and there were two branches coming off it pointing up to the third and fourth fingers of Apollo and Mercury. Despite her lack of qualifications, Tracey was no fool and those two branches showed achievement.

She had a success line and a strong line of ambition running up inside the lifeline to the base of the first finger of Jupiter. The curve of her hand showed talent and Tracey confessed to an aptitude for drawing. In addition to all these good qualities, Tracey's thumb was strong with even phalanges. She clearly had the drive and persistence to put all that ambition to good use.

> 'Tracey,' I said at last. 'You're not only going to get a job. You're going to do extremely well. You have the ability to run your own business and whatever you choose to do is going to be a success.'

Well, naturally Tracey was very pleased to hear this, but it all seemed a bit fantastic to a girl who was currently on the dole. It must have seemed as if I was spinning her a fairy tale.

Yet gradually things improved. Tracey found a job at last as an assistant in a dress shop. She'd always been interested in fashion and as she looked through the clothes day after day she realised that she could improve on some of the designs. She could even dream up more interesting garments herself she was sure.

The job gave her the confidence to enrol for evening classes in dress-making and design. While other girls went out night after night to the disco, Tracey stayed at home and worked. Her own talent and ambition did the rest.

Soon, practically everything Tracey wore was made to her own design. Occasionally customers in the shop remarked on what she was wearing and asked where she bought it. As for her friends, they were so impressed they wanted Tracey to make copies for them too. Within two years she had so many orders, she was able to give up her job and start her own business. Not long afterwards Tracey had made enough money to open her own shop and workroom with a team of machinists.

The last I heard of her she'd gone into partnership with

another woman and they were planning to open a shop in the West End.

> 'One day, Bettina, we'll have a chain of shops,' said Tracey.

And I'm sure they will. It just shows that ambition can help you overcome a poor start, no matter how bleak the prospects may seem.

Ambition, of course shows clearly on the palm but there are several variations to the line of the ambition.

The most straightforward are the lines like Tracey's which start inside the lifeline and reach up to the base of the first finger of Jupiter. (See Fig 9[d]) This shows an ambitious person who is unlikely to be influenced by others unless it is to his own advantage. If this line is accompanied by a strong success line ending under the third finger of Apollo, the owner will go straight to the top.

Sometimes the line of ambition veers towards the second finger of Saturn. This usually means frustration where ambition is concerned. The subject will have to overcome a number of obstacles before his ambitions are achieved.

Strangely enough I have also seen this type of line in the hands of medical students awaiting exam results and people expecting promotion. In these cases the line shows that ambition is bound up with a big effort already made, the outcome of which now rests with others.

If there is also a success line ending under Apollo, the subject is likely to pass his exams or gain the promotion he seeks. When the line of ambition ends between the fingers of Saturn and Apollo it means that the subject will have to achieve his ambitions entirely through his own work. There will be no help from anyone else.

Many people have no line of ambition at all. This may show that they have achieved their ambitions and are busy doing what they've always wanted to do or it can show that these people have no real ambition as far as material success is concerned. They are happy in a routine job finding fulfilment outside their career.

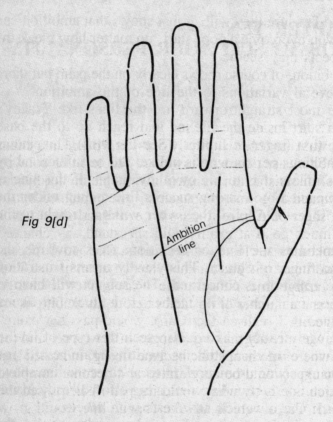

Fig 9[d]

Ambition
line

CHAPTER TEN:
A JOB TO SUIT YOUR PERSONALITY

Carol's story

Carol was a smart, beautifully dressed worker in a chain store. She wasn't content however. The tell-tale cobweb lines of dissatisfaction were plainly visible on her hands. She wanted to go into management she explained but to do so she would have to pass an exam and she'd never been much good at exams. Did she stand any chance?

I looked more closely at her hands. She had a success line and next to it was another line set at an angle. This was a change line. Close to the success line the change line was faint but a little further on it stuck out like a sore thumb. I realised that Carol would pass her exam.

She was already making changes in her career and the place where the change line became strong, indicated that the changes would be accelerated and become complete — which is exactly what would happen if she passed the exam. If Carol were to fail the change line would grow fainter not stronger and would eventually disappear altogether. Carol was very encouraged to hear this news. The last I heard she'd passed her exams and was now deputy manager of the store. (See Fig 10[a])

Changes in a career are always shown by these small lines and if the lines are strong and pointing up towards the fingers it generally means that the changes are for the better.

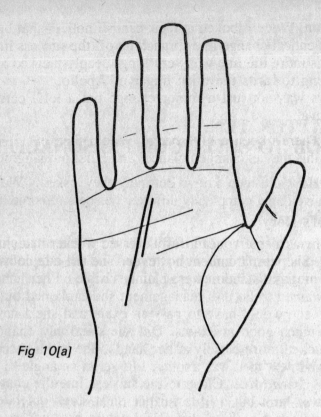

Fig 10[a]

If however the change line is accompanied by a break in the success line and the success line does not continue after the break, the change is unlikely to be beneficial and if you have any choice in the matter you should think very carefully before going ahead.

Occasionally I've seen identical change lines in two people who worked together. One married couple Alec and Nell ran a successful greengrocer's shop. The business had flourished over the years and there was every reason to suppose it would continue to do so until they retired.

Yet they decided to change direction completely. They gave up the shop and took over a pub in fashionable North

London. When I looked at their hands I noticed that both had identical change lines branching off the success line. What's more the line was very long, deeply marked and pointing towards the third finger of Apollo.

This was not just a minor change but a total career upheaval.

'There's been a big change,' I told them.
At this they exchanged glances and burst out laughing.

'How did you know Bettina?' they asked. 'We've given up a completely different business to come into this pub.'

I knew things would go well for them and to this day the pub is popular and well attended and the couple have never regretted their change of business.

Suitable careers

Below we provide a brief checklist to help you match your talents with an appropriate career.

● **Writer.**

- The fingers would be fairly long for detail.
- The head line would have a slight slope, indicating imagination and concentration.
- Also in some writer's hands, the headline ends in three branches, which is known as the writer's fork.
- The life line sweeps in a wide curve round the mount of Venus showing an ability to communicate with people.

107

- The thumb would be stiff, indicating a stubborn nature. A writer must persevere to the end of his manuscript.

- The second phalange of the thumb would be long showing a logical mind. This is necessary for arranging a mass of material in correct order.

● Dentist.

- Hand shape could be mixed.

- Good straight headline, combined with a straight heart line showing concentration, and patience.

- The thumb would be flexible showing a cool, detached nature.

- The palm would be elastic and springy, rather than stiff, since the dentist needs to be dexterous.

- The mount of Venus would be neither too full, nor too narrow, this shows a person who gets on well with others but doesn't become emotionally involved.

● Engineer.

- The spatulate hand, which is large and broad, with blunt finger tips, and knotty fingers, or a square hand.

- There are also those who have a slender yet spatulate hand. Often seen in electronics.

- Long fingers for love of detail.

- A long and sloping headline indicating imagination which is needed in this field.

- The long fingers would be rather flexible. The thumb partially waisted denoting a very logical mind.

- The success line and sun line could run together.
- The finger tips would be hard, the centre of the palm would be rather springy indicating a thoughtful nature.

● **Stockbroker.**

- Like those found in most business hands, the fingers would be long, showing a love of detail.
- The joints of the fingers would be knotty indicating shrewdness.
- The first phalange of the first finger of Jupiter would be long, showing willingness to take calculated risks.
- A long straight headline, denoting an analytical approach.
- Instead of a traditional straight success line, the stockbroker would have a line which is broken in places, under the finger of Apollo, showing the many different fields with which he has to deal.

● **Investment banker.**

- A square palm showing a capable, pratical nature.
- Rounded finger tips, indicating someone who is suited to dealing with money.
- The outer side of the hand would be slightly curved, showing creativity.
- A long small finger of Mercury revealing persuasive powers.

- A very strong success line ending under the second finger of Saturn since it is a very difficult job and the subject would have to struggle for success.

● Beautician.

- The skin texture would be soft, also the finger tips.

- The hand would narrow and feminine, with long pointed fingers, showing an artistic nature and love of beauty.

- The headline would slope down slightly, indicating imagination.

- The outer side of the hand would be curved denoting an artistic nature.

- The love line would sweep in a wide curve round the mount of Venus showing a love of people.

● Accountancy.

- Long fingers denoting a methodical mind, the phalanges would be even and the fingers straight.

- A long, straight intellectual headline.

- A straight heartline running across the hand rather than rising towards the fingers, indicating patience and concentration.

- The outer side of the hand would be straight showing a logical mind.

- The phalanges of the thumb would be even, indicating a balance between the will and reason.

- A strong line of intuition would be useful.

○ **Lawyer.**

– Long fingers indicating love of detail, and a square palm, rounded, square or even spatulate fingertips.

– The outer side of the hand would be straight, indicating a logical rather than creative mind.

– The headline would be straight and long, showing a logical, methodical mind, reliability and a good memory.

– The finger of Jupiter is usually long.

– The phalanges of the fingers would be even and well balanced.

– The first phalange of the thumb would be strong, the second phalange, which represents reason, slightly longer and well developed.

○ **Actors and Actresses.**

– The outer side of the hand would have a curve showing creativity.

– The headline would be slightly sloping denoting imagination.

– The small finger of Mercury would be fairly long indicating the ability to project a personality.

– The first finger of Jupiter would be long, showing a love of the limelight.

– A sloping line crossing the success line. This is often found in the hands of actors and actresses and also people who are highly gregarious.

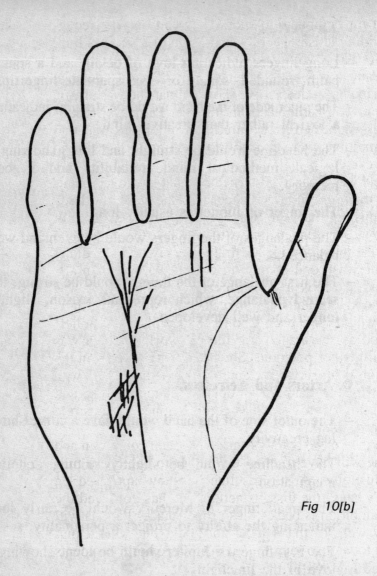

Fig 10[b]

- In addition to these qualities if the finger tips are firm, the subject doesn't like to take artistic direction and would be better to think of a career the other side of the spotlights; producer, director etc.

- Actresses' hands are long and slender, often having a stiff thumb, indicating the subject can at times be rather stubborn.

- The hands are soft, fingers long, indicating love of beautiful things.

● **Artists**

One of the most artistic hands I've ever seen belonged to artist and sculptor Ernest Leonard Smith – known as 'Schmidt'. His palm was very broad and square and there was a tremendous curve at the side of his palm. (See Fig 10[b])

I told him that he was very gifted and I discovered later that he designed (among other things) many Ascot Gold Cups and also the George Cross and the Star of Burma order for the late Lord Louis Mountbatten. His work can be seen in the silverwork of the RAF Chapel in Westminster Abbey and in Queen Mary's Dolls House at Windsor Castle.

Yet for all his achievements Ernest was a modest man. His very soft fingertips showed a quiet, retiring nature and I wasn't surprised to learn that he'd turned down an award of the M.V.O. for his work on the George Cross and the Star of Burma.

CHAPTER ELEVEN:
APPOINTING THE RIGHT STAFF

My old friends Charles and Marian were going through
a bad patch. They'd always been a devoted couple but
now they seemed to argue all the time. It was obvious
that something was wrong. As tactfully as I could I asked
if there was any particular problem bothering them.

At first they tried to laugh it off because they didn't
want to burden me with their worries, but finally Marian
admitted that it would be nice to talk to someone outside
the family.

It seemed that their hotel business which had been
booming for some years had suddenly taken a downturn
for no apparent reason. Bookings were as good as ever
but the takings were dropping and neither Marian nor
Charles could find out why. You didn't need to be clair-
voyant to work out that someone was cheating them
somewhere.

'The trouble is Bettina,' said Marian. 'We've got over
twenty staff now. How can we possibly tell if it's
one of them?'

'A palmist could tell,' I said.

'Maybe,' said Charles, 'but neither of us is a
palmist.'

'Well why don't I come down and look at their
hands?' I suggested.

Marian thought it was a marvellous idea. Most people are fascinated when they hear I read palms and if I visited the hotel as a guest of Marian and Charles, Marian felt sure it wouldn't be long before the staff were queueing up to show me their hands. The important thing was not to arouse suspicion. It must not look as if the owners were anxious for their staff to consult me.

There were three people besides Marian and Charles who handled money and we agreed that I should make them top priority. The plan went ahead perfectly. The only problem was that the guests wanted a turn too and I was kept busy for hours.

Yes, the plan worked well enough but my theory seemed on the verge of collapse. The three members of staff who handled money turned out to have honest, conscientous hands. I couldn't believe that any of them was untrustworthy

By this time of course I had a waiting list of eager clients and I couldn't disappoint them. I worked steadily through the afternoon. Then unexpectedly I came across two suspicious characters. A boy and a girl. Both members of staff.

The girl had a crooked little finger and her palm was spongey to touch with an unpleasant clammy feel. All signs of a potentially dishonest personality. The boy had stumpy fingers, his headline was short and the lower phalanges of his fingers were far longer than the top two, showing that he was more sensual than intellectual. Both his little finger of Mercury and third finger of Apollo were twisted. This young man was not too bright but he would be prepared to lie and cheat.

I couldn't prove anything of course but I was convinced that this pair had something to do with the hotel's misfortunes. I was busy until the early evening but at last I got the chance to talk privately to Marian and Charles. I warned them to keep an eye on the couple.

'That boy never gets near the money,' said Marian.

But then she remembered that when they were short staffed or particularly busy, the girl often helped out on the till.

'Right. We'll let her carry on,' said Charles, 'but we'll watch her.'

A few weeks later Marian and Charles invited me over for a special dinner. They were delighted. It seemed they had caught the girl taking money from the till and passing it to the boy who turned out to be her lover. The couple were dismissed on the spot and from that moment the takings rose dramatically.

It's rarely possible to examine a person's palm when they come for an interview for a job but you can often spot an untrustworthy character from the shape of his hands. Steer clear of people with the following characteristics:

- Crooked fingers are a classic sign of a deceitful nature, though you must be careful that the fingers are naturally twisted and not distorted as the result of an accident.

- When the little finger of Mercury is also bent like a claw, it reveals a born liar.

- A heavy, bulbous thumb suggests an aggressive nature which might make things difficult at work and a thumb that is excessively waisted belongs to a person who will do anything to get to the top and that includes anything illegal. You certainly wouldn't want them doing your accounts.

- Should a candidate have a first finger of Jupiter as

long as the second finger of Saturn, be careful. He wants to lead and he could push you out of a job.

● When the first finger is short however and the first phalange short, the subject will hate any form of criticism and will be inclined to sulk.

● It's a good idea to shake hands with potential employees as they leave. They might fake a firm handshake, but they won't be able to hide unusually soft skin, indicative of a sly and lazy nature, a leathery hand, suggesting callousness and a devious approach or a spongey palm showing a tendency to dishonesty.

The conscientious, honest worker will have long, straight fingers with even phalanges and if the job requires creative gifts he or she should also have a curved edge to the outside of the palm showing talent.

Checklist for choosing your staff

Most employers agree that choosing the right staff is a vital, yet extremely difficult task. Getting it wrong can prove to be costly and time consuming and in the case of certain key personnel a mistake can even turn out to be devastating to the company.

The problem is in fitting the right person into the right post. Naturally you want to employ staff who are honest and hard-working, but beyond that, each job will require different skills.

Someone who is over-qualified for a position could turn out to be just as inefficient at his job as someone who is under-qualified and it is pointless putting a high flyer into a routine post with few prospects or an artistic person into an area which requires a methodical, technical brain.

The unhappy misfit will soon leave and you'll have to start all over again.

This is where palmistry can help. A quick glance at the staff checklist below will help you isolate the important elements required in a range of important jobs.

Honesty:

Positive traits:
Straight fingers, phalanges that are even in size and shape. A firm handshake. Pleasantly dry skin.
Negative traits:
Crooked fingers, uneven phalanges, small finger of Mercury twisted or bent.
NB. Not to be confused with fingers distorted through accident or a small finger which curves slightly inwards towards the other fingers. This reveals a person who is unusually close to his grandparents.

Ability to work unsupervised:

Positive traits:
This will be an independent person whose headline begins some distance from the start of the lifeline. They will also have a stiff thumb showing the ability to stick at a task without giving up.
Negative traits:
The person who needs constant supervision has a headline which is joined to the lifeline for some distance. They have a weak thumb and the finger of Saturn could well be short signifying a frivolous temperament.

Creativity:

Positive traits:
A good curve on the outside of the hand showing artistic talent and a headline which slopes slightly downwards revealing a good imagination.
Negative traits:
The edge of the palm is straight and so is the headline. This is the sign of a technical mind and a person who prefers to work with facts.

A good team member:

Positive traits:
A wide gap separating the headline and heartline denoting a good sense of humour. A full mount of Venus (formed by the lifeline sweeping in a wide arc round the base of the thumb) showing a love of people and a long small finger of Mercury revealing a good communicator.
Negative traits:
The reverse of all these characteristics. Narrow gap between heart and headlines, thin mount of Venus and possibly a heavy thumb revealing a bad temper.

Plodder:

Positive traits:
Most firms need at least one plodder on the staff, someone who is content to work his way through monotonous tasks without getting bored. Small hands, average headline ending under the second finger of Saturn and crossing the palm without sloping show-

ing average intelligence and little imagination. No lines of ambition and no success line. Straight side to the palm

Negative traits:
Long first finger of Jupiter revealing a wish to lead. Clear ambition lines rising from within the lifeline and leading to the base of Jupiter. A distinct curve to the hand showing creative talent and a stiff, determined thumb.

Good salesman: *Positive traits:*
Long small finger of Mercury revealing a charming and persuasive talker. Long second finger of Saturn showing ability to weigh up situations quickly. A flexible thumb with the tip turned back and a strong second phalange emphasising persuasive powers. Possibly bends in the fingers as the salesman might need to 'bend' the truth on occasions.

Negative traits:
Stiff thumb and very straight fingers showing a stubborn adherence to the truth even if it's not to his advantage. Headline and lifeline joined revealing a cautious nature.

Hard worker: *Positive traits:*
The hand will feel hard in texture, the mount of Venus will be narrow and the headline will run straight across the palm without sloping. The fingers

are likely to be thin. This is the sign of a person who puts work before pleasure and will work very hard.

Negative traits:

A soft, broad, fleshy hand with a full mount of Venus revealing a sensuous, generous nature. The second finger of Saturn may be short denoting a frivolous approach to life and work. This is the sign of the person who regrets that work stands in the way of his social life.

Flexibility:

Positive traits:

Flexible fingers and a thumb that bends back from the tips. Good headline and a heartline that curves up towards the fingers. This shows a tolerant, adaptable character who will have a go at anything.

Negative traits:

Stiff fingers and thumb showing a rigid attitude inclined to stubborness. Possibly a short small finger of Mercury revealing a tendency to stick to the letter of his job description.

Management potential:

Positive traits:

The first finger of Jupiter will be almost as long as the second finger of Saturn revealing leadership qualities. A good headline, fairly long and separated from the lifeline at the beginning showing confidence and intelligence. The phalanges would be even, heart and headline well separated indicating a sense of humour and a slight curve to the side of the hand showing creativity. The small finger of Mercury would be long revealing a good communicator.

Negative traits:

The opposite of the above. Short fingers of Saturn and Jupiter. Possibly a wide palm and fingers revealing a sensuous nature or a heavy thumb hinting at a tendency to lose his temper easily. Heart and headlines close together showing a lack of humour and a certain narrowness of mind.

Ability to teach others:

Positive traits:

Long, slim fingers, the ends rounded, spatulate or square. A long headline showing a good mind. A medium full mount of Venus revealing a warm-hearted nature but not a pushover. Long first finger of Jupiter showing leadership ability. Long small finger of Mercury denoting a good com-municator and an independent headline.

Negative traits:

The opposite of the above. In par-ticular a short first finger of Jupiter, headline joined to the lifeline and a short finger of Mercury. This shows a shy, quiet individual who doesn't like to push himself forward and finds it difficult to talk to people he doesn't know very well.

Building a team

Naturally another consideration when employing staff who have to work in close proximity to each other, is will they get on? It's no good having workers who are brilliant at their jobs if they dissipate energy which should go into their work on pointless personality clashes.

That indefinable chemistry which exists between good friends, or even bitter enemies is very hard to pin down, the best you can do is stick to some general rules and hope for the best.

You won't go far wrong if you look for staff who share that valuable wide gap between heart and headlines which tells of a good sense of humour and a broad minded outlook. If they also tend to have long small fingers of Mercury they are good communicators too and a full mount of Venus shows that they like people. Staff with these characteristics will get on with most people and are therefore likely to work well together.

It's a good idea to steer clear of candidates with heavy, bulbous thumbs. They may turn out to be quarrelsome with a violent temper if pushed too far. It would also be as well not have too many staff with Jupiter fingers which are markedly long. Too many born leaders struggling for dominance is not good for harmony in the work place.

How to spot a conman

Finally, how can you tell if the plausible character in front of you is really a conman?

The first test is the handshake. The conman's handshake is limp, the skin texture unusually soft and the hand rather clammy. Most of the time the conman prefers to keep his hands in his pockets. He has something to hide and unconsciously reveals his secretive nature even while his manner is apparently open and friendly.

When you do get a glimpse of his hands the fingers are likely to be twisted, the thumb very flexible with a waisted appearance and the small finger of Mercury is probably extremely long. This man can charm his way out of any uncomfortable situation but you can't believe a word he says.

Motivating force

Everyone needs motivation to give of their best at work. but different people respond to different things. The obvious incentive is money of course in the form of commission or bonus payments or merit rises. Yet surprisingly enough, this doesn't work well with everyone. Few people would actually turn down extra money but, equally some wouldn't put themselves to a great deal of trouble to gain it.

There are people for example who are desperately seeking praise and appreciation and a few kind words will have more effect than a few pounds in their pay packet. Others want power and status and will do anything for an important sounding title and the key to the executive washroom.

The problem is how to tell which person responds to which incentive. Well, a glance at their hands will give you a pretty good idea. Money oriented people tend to have fingers set close together on the hand. Their fingers are often long and pointed and the little finger of Mercury leans slightly towards the third finger of Apollo.

People who respond well to praise are often lacking in self esteem. Their first finger of Jupiter is rather short and the little finger of Mercury leans slightly away from the other fingers. If you could see the lines on their palm the chances are that the headline would be joined to the lifeline or would start very close to it. Power seekers on the other hand have a long first finger of Jupiter and often their fingers are short.

Finally: are you a good boss?

The perfect boss from the employees' point of view would be kind, fair, tactful and diplomatic. These qualities would show up in a full mount of Venus and a strong heartline which ends under or near the first finger of Jupiter, a long, straight headline and a strong thumb with equal phalanges.

Nobody is perfect of course, but the closer your hand comes to this description the better your staff will like you.

CHAPTER TWELVE:
SHOULD YOU GO INTO
PARTNERSHIP?

Val was an attractive dark-haired lady. Her face was full of quiet intelligence and her fingers had knotty joints which proved that she was shrewd as well as clever. Val was a business woman and she was about to make a decision which would affect her business. Without giving me any clues, could I tell her whether the outlook was good or bad, she wanted to know.

To answer such a question, the first thing I tend to look at is the success line. When I looked at Val's I realised straight away what step she was considering. Down near the base of her palm where the success line started, I saw three lines that merged into one to form the success line. These lines leapt out at me. They showed very clearly that Val was going into partnership with three other people. (See Fig 12[a])

Unfortunately things were not going to be perfect. One of the partner lines twisted back and up and pointed towards the little finger of Mercury which influences money and worldly affairs. This partner would prove to be a very bad choice and would probably cheat Val financially. Apart from this, the signs were good.

She was amazed when I told her this but non committal about her plans. She had been intending to go into partnership with three men but now she was in a difficult position. I had been able to tell her that one of the partners was an unwise choice. The problem was I couldn't say which one.

Well, Val went ahead with the partnership but some months later she wrote to me. Apparently I'd been absolutely right. One of the partners had been untrustworthy where money was concerned and she had been forced to part company with him. Since then the business had been doing extremely well and they were expanding.

As a rule I'm wary about partnerships. At the beginning when your setting up in business it's often very comforting to share the problems and hopes with another party, but so often as the enterprise gets established, the relationship goes wrong.

I don't know why it is but as soon as money arrives, the best of friends can fall out. One partner can feel that he is making more effort than the other. Resentments grow and when there is a lot of money at stake people can turn out to be less honest than you have ever suspected.

Partnerships often show up on the palm in the form of branches at the base of the success line, each branch corresponding to one partner. If the partnership is a good one, the success line will run straight to the third finger of Apollo or the fourth finger of Mercury indicating great success.

If the partnership is a disaster, the success line will often fade out altogether showing that you are never going to get anywhere in business with this particular person. Dishonest partners are revealed by a partner line which twists or turns.

This is all very well of course, but it's not much help in choosing the right partner. So many people seem honest, amiable and hard working when you meet them, only to turn into quite the opposite when you've been in close contact for six months.

And even if the partner turns out to be honest and

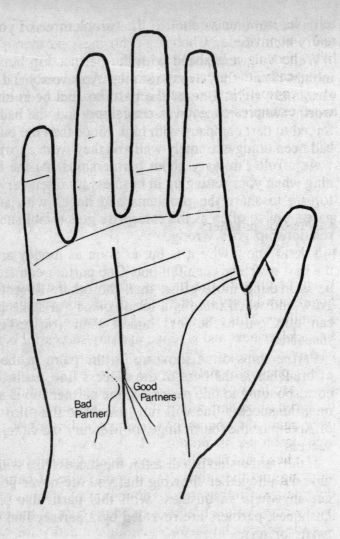

Bad Partner

Good Partners

Fig 12[a]

reliable, how can you tell if the two or three of you are really compatible? Choosing a business partner is a bit like choosing a husband or wife.

Basically, the greater the similarity in your hands, the more compatible you are likely to be. Below I've given some examples of good partnerships.

Successful partners

Fig 12[b]

If we begin with the fingers, note that the two middle fingers are knotty on the joints giving the appearance of a swelling. This is a good sign indicating shrewdness in financial matters and is found in many successful business hands.

The phalanges between the fleshy parts of the finger joints are fairly even, again a good sign revealing a well balanced mind and personality. The thumb is strong and once again the phalanges are equal indicating that will and reason are in proportion.

The head and heartlines have a nice gap between them showing that the subject has a good sense of humour, a definite asset in business. The mount of Venus, created by the curve of the lifeline around the base of the thumb, is wide which shows warmth and sympathy for others.

The success line traces its way up the palm and a shadow of the sun line is beginning to appear which indicates a change for the better in a business venture. The owner of this hand has a good business brain and gets on well with others. He or she would make an ideal partner.

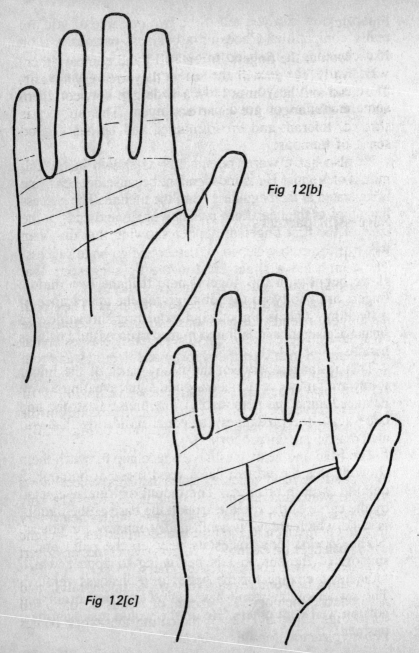

Fig 12[b]

Fig 12[c]

Fig 12[c]

If we look at the fingers in Fig 12[b] and compare them with Fig 12[c] you will notice that they are very similar. The head and heartlines have a wide gap between them and the phalanges are clear and even. This subject is shrewd, tolerant and broad-minded and he has a good sense of humour.

He also has a warm personality as shown in his full mount of Venus. He is independent because his head line is separated at the beginning from the lifeline. The success line stops at the heartline, picks up again and ends at the base of the first finger of Jupiter showing that this man will overcome obstacles in his career and go on to success. The thumb has a slight bend at the tip suggesting that he reasons things out and plans carefully.

These two would make excellent partners. They both have open, friendly dispositions and share a keen sense of humour. There should be no personality clashes a vital consideration in any partnership. In addition they are both natural businessmen who will make a success of any venture they undertake. The firmness and flexibility of Fig 12[c] revealed in his thumb will compensate for the hint of stubbornness suggested in the thumb of Fig 12[b].

Fig 12[d]

A very strong hand which indicates that this subject knows what he wants and no-one will stand in his way. The only weakness is shown by the first finger of Jupiter being very thin in comparison to the others and rather long, but the even phalanges on each of the fingers overcomes any overt bossiness which could irritate others.

The long headline reveals very good concentration and a wonderful memory. The mount of Venus is not so full as in Figs 12[a] and 12 [b] indicating that work comes before pleasure for this subject.

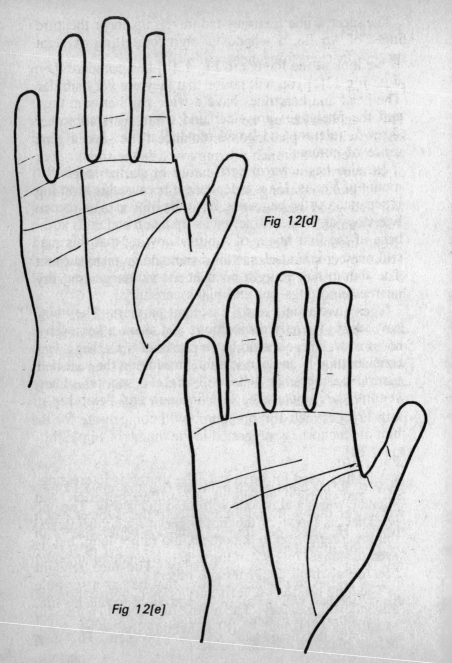

Fig 12[d]

Fig 12[e]

The success line is strong and travels up under the third finger of Apollo, a wonderful sign foretelling of great success in everything he does.

Fig 12[e]

This is another strong, heavy hand. The fingers are rather knotty with the phalanges in balance. The success line is followed by a branch veering towards the small finger of Mercury showing a new career or partnership.

The thumb is strong and rather stiff revealing a strong will and good reasoning powers though a tendency to stubbornness.

The mount of Venus is similar to that of Fig 12[d]. This subject would want things to be done in the correct way with proper procedures adhered to. He is also very hardworking.

These two would make good partners. Both share a disciplined approach to work as shown by the smaller mount of Venus and well-developed head-lines. Fig 12[e] stubborn thumb shows that he will not be pushed around and this would enable him to cope with Fig 12[d] tendency to dominate, displayed in that long, thin finger of Jupiter. Both are destined for success.

Fig 12[f]

A very fine hand for business. The thumb is interesting. Stiff and upright it shows great determination and willpower that will undoubtedly help this subject reach the top. He has strong lines of ambition which rise from inside the lifeline to the base of the first finger of Jupiter revealing an ambitious personality. The nice straight fingers and even phalanges prove that he has a sensible disposition and will not allow his ambitions to rule his life.

The fingers are long indicating that he pays great attention to detail and analyses every problem. This man

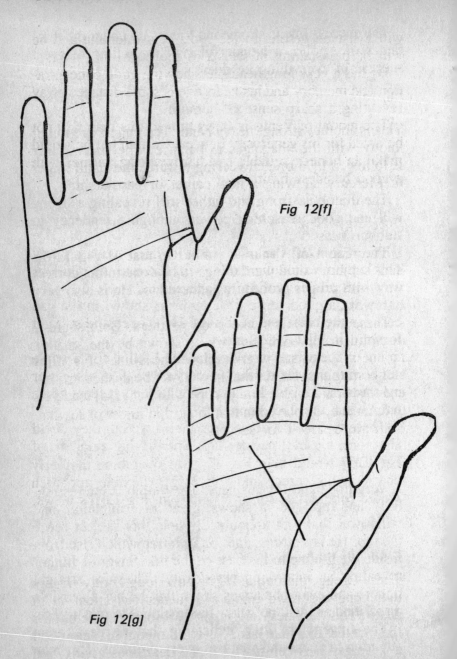

Fig 12[f]

Fig 12[g]

will insist on getting to the roots of a dilemma and he will be painstaking in search of the truth.

He has a very long headline, showing good concentration and memory and his heart line is some distance away revealing a sharp sense of humour.

The mount of Venus is fairly thin so this man will not be noted for his generosity or great warmth but he would make an honest, reliable and hardworking partner with a good business brain.

Fig 12[g]

Unlike Fig 12[f] the owner of this hand has a slightly supple thumb showing that he will listen to the opinions of others and is willing to take advice.

He has a good sense of humour as shown in the gap between the heart and headlines. He is open and straight forward in all his dealings.

The success line is joined by the lifeline for a while suggesting that for a time he was held back in his career by domestic affairs, but independence and success come later when the lines separate.

These two would do well on their own but they could also form a useful partnership. The driving ambition of Fig 12[f] would help Fig 12[g] to overcome the early check in his career and Fig 23[g]'s flexible approach would compensate for any rigidity in Fig 12[f]'s views.

Fig 12[h]

These strong, masculine hands have long knotty fingers indicating a shrewd mind and meticulous attention to detail. This 'fussiness' might jar with some people but for the fact that this man has a very full mount of Venus and a wide gap between his head and heartlines giving him

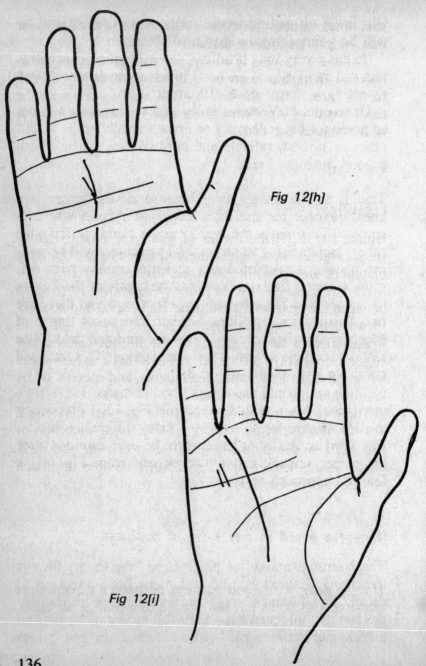

Fig 12[h]

Fig 12[i]

such a warm personality and attractive sense of humour that people are drawn to him.

The line of success is broken and then joins again showing that there has been or will be some major setback in his career. But the branch line heading towards the third finger of Apollo suggests that tremendous success will come in the end.

Fig 12[i]

This is an interesting hand because all the fingers are knotty except for the third finger of Apollo which is smooth. This makes the Apollo finger stand out from the others emphasising its strength. The subject will be willing to take a calculated risk and this usually pays off.

The success line rises towards the centre of the fingers of Apollo and Mercury, an excellent sign and there are two smaller success lines beneath the small finger of Mercury showing success in two unconnected fields. The sloping headline reveals a fine imagination. This man will come up with plenty of ideas.

These two would make very good partners. Fig 12[h]'s meticulous brain would overcome Fig 12[i]'s tendency to rush about trying to set up too many different ventures. Fig 12[h] on the other hand might be over cautious after his career setback and would benefit from Fig 12[i]'s fearless approach to risks.

Types to avoid in any form of business

Having dealt with good partners perhaps it's even more important to point out the people to avoid at all costs.

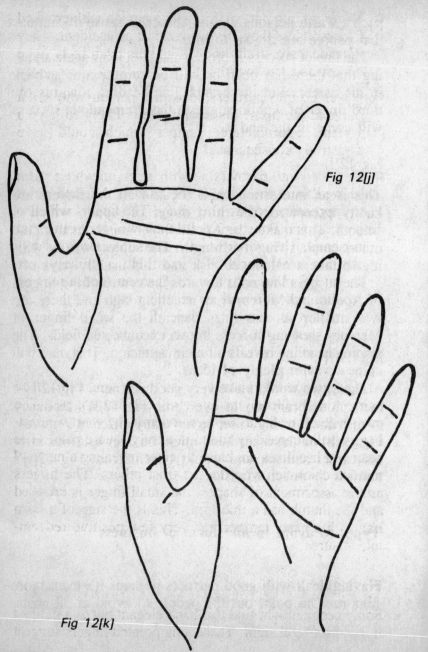

Fig 12[j]

Fig 12[k]

● Never go into partnership with a person with crooked fingers unless they are the result of an accident. They indicate a sly, crafty individual who is unlikely to be honest and trustworthy.

● Never go into partnership with a person who has a bulge at the tip of his thumb. He is likely to have a violent, unpredictable temper which could have disastrous consequences.

● Never go into partnership with a person whose palm viewed from the back of the hand is thin and gives the appearance of wasting away. The fingers will also be long and bony and the thumb will turn out from the hand. The owner of such a hand is a dreamer living in a small world of his own. He is unlikely ever to put his plans into action. Take on such a man or woman and you will do all the work.

Fig 12[j]

At first glance this palm appears to be square in shape but look more closely and you will see that it is not. The outer side of the hand slopes in towards the wrist weakening the solid capability found in a truly square palm. The heart and headlines are close together revealing a narrow minded character who doesn't trust others. The fingers are an assortment of shapes, the small finger is crooked and the thumb has a thick tip. This is the sign of a born liar with a nasty temper and very few positive redeeming features.

Fig 12[k]

Some people might find this hand elegant but to a palmist it is a distasteful sight. These long pointed fingers suggest

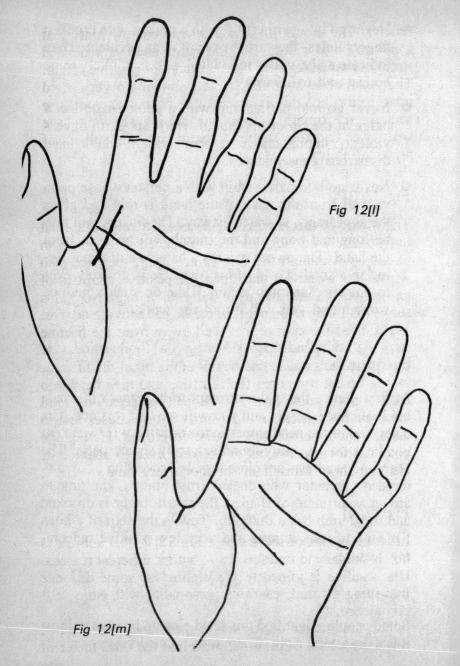

Fig 12[l]

Fig 12[m]

cruelty. The mount of Venus is very narrow hinting at a selfish, cold nature and the palm itself is long and shapeless revealing very little aptitude for positive action. The headline is long and sloping showing a very vivid imagination but this is unlikely to be put to good use because the thumb is thin and sloping showing little willpower and that shapeless palm robs the subject of practical ability.

Fig 12 [l]

The owner of this hand is not necessarily unpleasant but unfortunately he lacks the qualities needed to get on in business. Although the fingers are long, they are also waisted, a weakness that turns the positive qualities of an analytical, meticulous mind into a negative. This subject is likely to be overcritical to an annoying degree.

The headline commences well away from the lifeline showing independence bordering on foolhardiness at times and the success line begins at the tip of the lifeline, moves on till it reaches the heartline and then begins to fade — not a good sign. This subject has plenty of good ideas but his critical yet over-hasty nature causes him to dismiss them before they can be developed. He has the potential for success but is unlikely ever to achieve it. He will shoot himself in the foot every time.

Fig 12[m]

Like the owner of the hand in Fig 12[l], this subject is highly unlikely to find success — but for different reasons. His headline is joined to the lifeline for some distance indicating a timid, cautious personality with little self-confidence.

The first finger of Jupiter is short and undeveloped revealing a lack of personal pride and the third finger of

Apollo and the small finger of Mercury lean in towards each other. Far from taking a risk this man would be willing to sacrifice his friends in order to save himself. This man would make an appalling partner in business or anything else.

CHAPTER THIRTEEN: SHOULD YOU DIVERSIFY?

No-one could deny Peter's energy. Peter was everywhere. Having made his money in the oil business he decided it was time to branch out. He went into jewellery, he bought race horses and took up racing in a serious way. Then his instincts told him that travel was the boom trade of the future so he invested in hotels overseas. And somehow, despite all this, he kept his oil company ticking over.

Peter of course was an intelligent man but no-one's superhuman. He had been coming to me from time to time over the years and one day when I looked at his palm I saw a change that spelled trouble.

Peter had always had a terrific success line. It ran arrow straight up to his palm to end under the third finger of Apollo and several smaller lines rested beside it under the same finger. This showed that Peter had the potential to be a great success in a number of different areas. And he was. (See Fig 13[a])

These lines had been present in Peter's hand throughout the years I'd known him but now when I looked at the familiar palm I saw something different. The mass of success lines had thinned out. Many had faded away altogether and a new line had appeared next to the success line. This line ran directly to the second finger of Saturn.

Any lines ending under this finger tell of problems and setbacks. There was clearly trouble ahead for Peter and

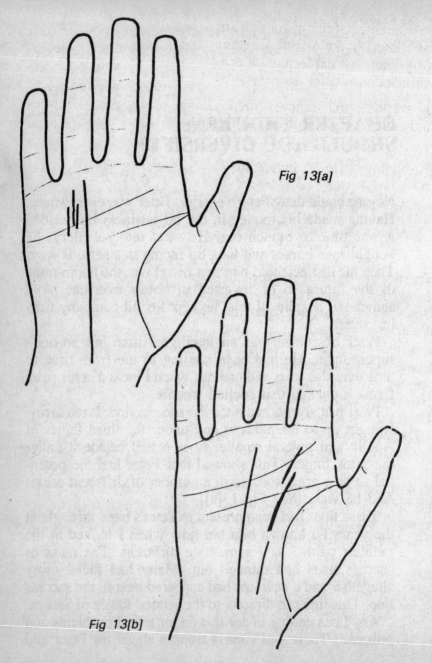

Fig 13[a]

Fig 13[b]

it was connected with his career since the setback line branched off from his success line. The fact that some of his smaller success lines had disappeared indicated that the problems would lead to a loss in the areas in which he had previously been successful. There were also fine stress lines showing on the palm.

'I think you're trying to do too much Peter,' I warned him. 'You're spreading yourself too thin.'

'Can't be helped love,' said Peter, 'I'll manage. I always do.'

I tried to warn him of problems ahead but he was confident he could handle anything that came up.

Six months later I heard that Peter's hotel venture had collapsed. He was unable to devote enough time and attention to hotel management and without his guidance things had gone wrong.

I have seen many similar cases where success seems to go to a person's head. They get greedy and think they can do anything. Sadly they often lose everything they've built up by this failure to recognise their limitations.

When you are thinking of diversifying it's a good idea to study your palm before committing yourself. A new venture in business will often show as a change line next to the success line starting between the headline and the heartlines and running up towards the first finger of Jupiter. (See Fig 13[b])

If this line runs clear and unbroken, the venture will be a success, but if another horizontal line cuts across it, the prospects are poor. You should think very carefully indeed about proceeding.

Should there be an island on the change line as well as a line bisecting it, frankly I'd forget the whole idea. The enterprise could turn out to be a disaster.

Will you recover from a setback?

No matter how careful you are, you can't eliminate problems altogether. Staff let you down, markets crumble, clients fail to pay . . . There is always something that can trip you up when you least expect it. It would take a remarkably lucky and optimistic man or woman to hope to avoid all setbacks throughout their career. The realistic businessman has to accept that setbacks will occur. The important point is, will he recover from them?

Naturally you need strength of character to overcome obstacles in any walk of life and this is shown in a strong, well developed thumb and even phalanges on the fingers. But when you are talking about business setbacks, there is another clue to look for. The formation of the success line.

A few years ago one of my clients came for a reading and I saw distinct signs of an impending setback in his hand. Albert V. Avey had worked very hard all his life and had established a promising packaging company. He was prepared to put in 24 hours a day if necessary to make a success of his business. Albert seemed to be doing everything right — and yet I could see problems ahead.

His success line rose up his hand towards the second finger of Saturn. This is not the best of signs, indicating that to reach success the subject will have to work very hard and overcome many obstacles. Worse still, the line came to a complete stop low down on Albert's hand. This foretold of a very serious setback indeed — one that could even put Albert out of business altogether.

Before alarming Albert unnecessarily, I searched around for something more hopeful and I found it. There, under the third finger of Apollo a new success line had started up. This short line took over from the original success line.

Albert was clearly going to face a very serious problem. Things would look extremely black, but he would

146

come through the bad patch and go on to do well. Naturally Albert received this news with mixed feelings. Particularly as he couldn't foresee any problem of such magnitude. Yet I was sure something was going to go wrong and that he should be prepared.

Not long after this, one of Albert's most valuable clients went broke owing him thousands of pounds. The loss was so serious that for a time Albert didn't know how he'd ever recover. But he remembered my words and instead of giving up he plodded on. He persuaded the bank to give him another chance, he worked seven days a week and eventually the business was restored to health. Today Albert is doing even better than ever. (See Figs 13[c] and [d])

The overseas connection

I think the woman was curious more than anything. There was no particular over-riding problem in her life. She came to me simply because she had heard about palmistry and she wondered what I would make of her hand. I sensed that she was quite sceptical when she arrived but that didn't bother me at all. I like working with sceptics. The look of amazement you often see on their faces as they leave makes me smile.

Anyway I noticed immediately that this woman had a pronounced curve to the side of her hand showing artistic talent and creativity. Did she paint by any chance? I asked. She said she did. It was only a hobby but she found it very relaxing to go into the country with her paints and easel and work away at watercolours for hours at a time.

The combination of artistic talent and a first class business brain is not all that common but when I studied her hand more closely I saw that the lady was born for business. A square palm, strong thumb, good head and heartlines, a well marked success line, shrewd knotty fingers . . . it was all there. Yet she wasn't in business.

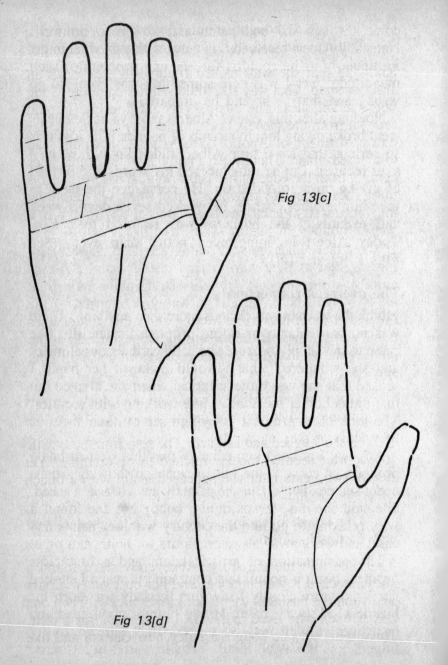

Fig 13[c]

Fig 13[d]

'I've often thought about it now you mention it Bettina,' she said, 'but I've never known what to do.'

Knowing that she was artistic I suggested she open an antiques shop. That way she could sell her paintings along with the antiques. The business would flourish, I could see that from the success line and the way it ended under the third finger of Apollo. What's more, it would lead to overseas trade. There were a number of horizontal lines coming from the edge of her palm right across her success line. These lines are known as travel lines. On their own they mean significant overseas journeys — not just a week's holiday in Spain. (See Fig 13[e])

When these lines are very strong and deep, almost joining together as they were on my client's hand it means either that the subject's job will take him abroad or that his work will be connected to foreign countries. If the lines start from inside the lifeline and other travel lines come across towards them from the opposite side of the palm it shows that the subject could even end up living abroad.

'Don't be surprised if you end up in the export business,' I told the woman.

Well she laughed and laughed. The leap from housewife to exporter seemed too far fetched to be credible. Yet nearly two years later she appeared again with a bunch of roses for me.

'I've come to apologise because I laughed at you Bettina,' she said.

Then she told me the story. Apparently she'd found a shop, stocked it with antiques and her best watercolours and soon the business was ticking over nicely. Then one day her son who lived in the USA came back for a visit. During his stay he bought a fancy new camera and like

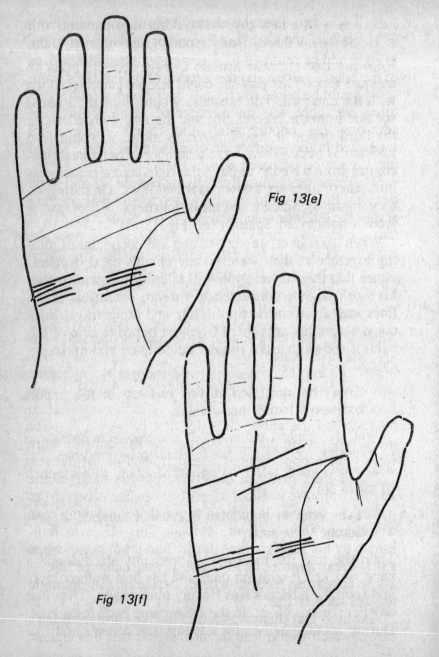

Fig 13[e]

Fig 13[f]

everyone with a new toy, he couldn't stop playing with it. He drove his family mad by photographing everything in sight and he returned to America with countless snaps of the house, garden and the interior of his mother's shop.

No doubt he bored his friends back home with his pictures but there was an unexpected result. Instead of admiring his photography, the friends were more interested in the antiques on display in the shop. Would his mother be prepared to sell them?

My client was naturally delighted to do so and soon a steady flow of antiques and watercolours was pouring across the Atlantic. Demand increased to such an extent that she had to compile a proper catalogue and now she is well and truly in the export business. (See Fig 13[f])

Ian's story

Another recent case involving a career overseas was a young man named Ian. He was a photographer working in London. He was doing well enough in a mundane sort of way but deep down I think he was bored. When I looked at his hand I saw that his success line started half-way up the palm, showing that he wouldn't make much progress in the early part of his life but that there were golden opportunities ahead. (See Fig 13[g])

Travel lines marched clearly across his hand. Some started from the outside edge of his palm, others from within the lifeline. It seemed to me that this young man would very soon be living abroad. This idea was reinforced by his success line. Hardly had it got going when a tiny break appeared and beside it was a change line — a line appearing from nowhere, beside and at an angle to, the success line.

I realised that there was a big change coming in Ian's career which would lead to success and that this change involved a foreign country. The change and travel lines were so strong it was likely that Ian would end up living and working abroad.

There was only one problem. A branch line ran from the success line and pointed towards the finger of Saturn showing temporary setbacks in his career. Any line pointing to Saturn suggests drawbacks and the fact that it came from the success line indicated that these would be connected to career.

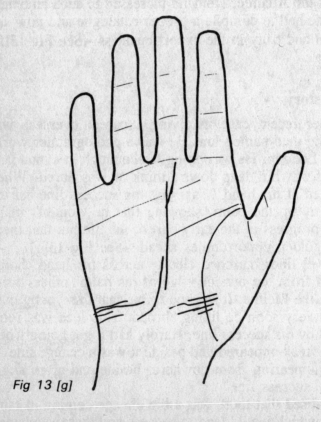

Fig 13 [g]

It turned out that Ian was thinking about going to Spain. I advised him to do so but not just yet. He should wait a month or two or there might be problems. Ian took my advice. Four months later when I saw him again, the setback line had vanished and his success line had sprouted a tassel like the head of a broom which showed that there were countless opportunities awaiting him.

Well, Ian went to Spain and it turned out that had he gone earlier he would have encountered a problem and would not have been able to meet the people who eventually helped him. Now he is juggling with at least three successful careers and looks set to go into television.

CHAPTER FOURTEEN: STRESS

We hear a lot about stress these days. Some people say it's a killer. Others tell us we'd achieve nothing without it. Well, I'm no expert but judging from the hands of people who come to see me, stress is not particularly beneficial. In fact I've met many people who were performing badly in their careers simply because they were under too much stress.

Stress grilles

Stress shows up unmistakably in the hand. No matter how calm a face the subject manages to put on, their palm will reveal the inner turmoil. Stress can be seen a a network of criss-cross lines like a chequer board on the palm. When things get really bad and the stress is having a detrimental effect on the career, islands form on the success line. This is a warning sign and must be taken seriously. (See Fig 14[a])

I advise anyone with this type of mark to take a break immediately or they could risk losing everything for which they've worked.

There are many reasons for stress. Sometimes the person concerned is taking on more work than is humanly possible, but often personal problems trigger the predicament. As domestic worries occupy their thoughts, business begins to slide, causing more worries which make the domestic problems worse and soon the subject is caught in a downward spiral.

One of my clients trapped in such a way was a clever woman who ran a cosmetic business. In the past the business had been very successful but now it was in trouble. I discovered afterwards that the lady was on the verge of ruin.

She possessed good business hands and a success line than ran straight to Apollo, yet she was in trouble and I could see it at a glance. Stress lines covered her palm In the middle of the success line was a large island and immediately after the island was a break, unguarded by any protective second line running parallel to it. See Fig 14[b])

If this lady continued the way she was going she would lose her business and that part of the success line which lay after the break would fade away altogether. I urged her in the strongest possible terms to take a holiday at once. This advice doesn't go down too well with business people. They're always too busy to go on holiday at a moments notice. They don't seem to realise that if they were ill or suffered an accident, they would be forced to take time off — so why not take a break as a preventive measure? It would save time in the long run.

Anyway on this occasion my client was in such a desperate position that she was ready to try anything. If I told her a holiday would help then she was prepared to take a holiday. She left for Vienna and a complete rest a few days later.

It was some months before I heard from her again. She wrote me a wonderful letter. Her life had improved out of all recognition since we'd met. While she was on holiday she relaxed and was able to look at her problems objectively. She realised that she had been diverting all her energy into sustaining a failing love affair and there had been nothing left over for her business. Inevitably

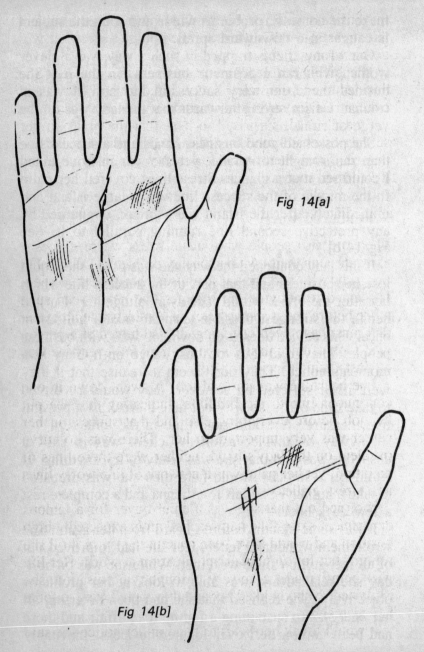

Fig 14[a]

Fig 14[b]

the business suffered but blinded by her emotions and the stress she was suffering, she couldn't see what was going wrong.

The break enabled her to sort out the muddle. She decided to end the stale relationship once and for all and concentrate on saving her business.

I wasn't at all surprised to hear that the break in her success line had knitted together and the island had disappeared. From then on her cosmetics company regained it's former success.

Self-induced worry

There are also people who create stress where it doesn't exist, through their own personality problems. I remember one lady who had the most unusual headline I've seen. It seemed to entwine the lifeline. I've never seen such a line before and it showed lack of confidence to an extent that must have been crippling. It also hinted at a person who took offence easily — since they felt everyone was against them. (See Fig 14[c])

The heartline was unusual too. It swept down in one continuous line to the headline, indicating that she put her job before everything else and that success in her career was very important to her. There was no curve of talent on the lady's hand, neither were there lines of ambition, yet her palm was a network of fine worry lines and stress grilles.

It turned out that she was a chief buyer for a famous department store. She had reached an unexpectedly high position and would have been content to stay in it till she retired, but for an unpleasant situation at work. Her life was being made a misery through victimisation she explained. Nobody liked her and they were trying to force her to resign.

It would break her heart to hand in her notice she said

157

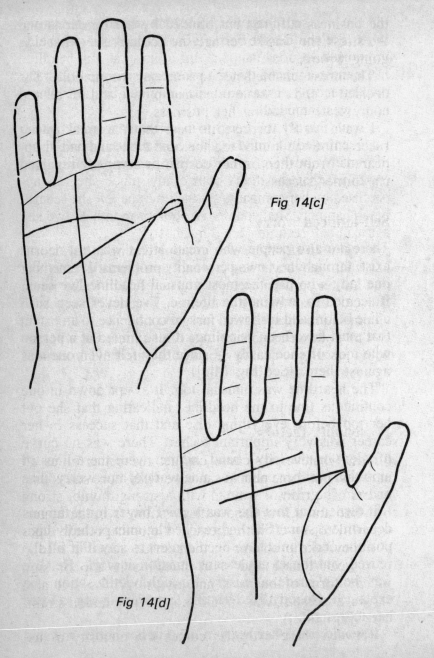

Fig 14[c]

Fig 14[d]

but she was so unhappy she couldn't see any alternative. Well, she could have been right. Perhaps she was being victimised. It does happen. But looking at that headline made me convinced that the problems stemmed from her own insecurity. I was sure she imagined hostility where none was intended.

I could hardly tell her this in so many words. Instead I concentrated on building her confidence. I pointed out the many positive qualities in her personality and explained that she didn't realise how much she was appreciated by her company. By the time she left she seemed much happier. She would wait another month or two she agreed, before doing anything hasty.

I'm glad to say there was a happy ending to this story. My client stayed in her job and some months later she met a man on a business trip. They fell in love, which boosted her confidence tremendously and all thoughts of victimisation disappeared for good.

If all goes well in her private life I expect she will stay in her job till she qualifies for a gold watch and a pension.

Personality factors

Stress, whatever it's cause can get the better of us all at times, but some people can cope with more stress than others. The man or woman with a strong thumb, strong headline and a firm hand with no softness in the fingertips will cope well with stress. Little bothers these types and they take problems in their stride. (See Fig 14[d])

A weak thumb and short headline is a poor sign in any form of business and not surprisingly it also shows a person who should not be put under strain. (See Fig 14[e])

Between these extremes comes the majority of us.

Basically, the firmer the hand the better as far as stress is concerned and the person with soft fingertips and 'elderly' looking palms covered in hundreds of tiny worry lines, is more suited to a tranquil life. Too much stress could make them ill.

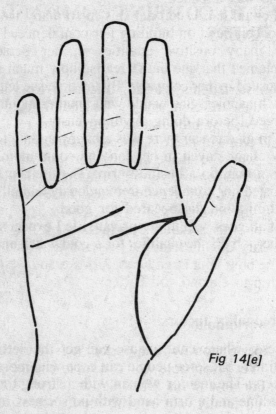

Fig 14[e]

CHAPTER FIFTEEN:
HOW TO COMBINE HOME AND BUSINESS

Simon started his working life as a lorry driver. He enjoyed the travelling and the freedom from an office desk but he was ambitious too. He saw no reason why he should work to make money for someone else when he could work to make money for himself. So Simon volunteered for every job that came in. He slaved seven days a week and eventually he'd raised enough money to buy his own lorry.

Simon was a natural business man. He had all the necessary qualities for success and he found it. Gradually he built up a large fleet of lorries and went into partnership to expand still further.

The workaholic

On paper Simon was the perfect rags to riches business story. Yet few people would want to change places with him. For now in his fifties Simon is alone. There is no wife, no family, not even a settled home.

To be fair, this doesn't seem to worry Simon overmuch. He had his chances but chose business success before personal happiness every time. Some years ago there was a woman who loved him but Simon could spare her little time. Their few dates were often cancelled at the last minute because of sudden crises at work and eventually she got tired of waiting and left him.

Somehow Simon couldn't seem to find the time for another relationship after that so he gave up on love altogether. As for a home, well Simon believes that's more a woman's province. He bought a house once because everybody said he should get into property but he was away most of the time and when he did get back he was lonely rattling around by himself. He sold the place and moved into his club.

Simon is not particularly unhappy. He is married to his business and he's a self sufficient man but not many people would willingly accept such a life, particularly as they get older.

The story highlights the problems that many encounter when they try to mix business with a happy domestic life. Business eats up time and energy which loving partners feel should be spent on them. The resulting broken marriages and relationships cause great distress, financial hardship in many cases and often, the kind of stress that is detrimental to the business which caused it in the first place.

There are some people who are probably best advised not to attempt a long term relationship at all. These are the workaholics. The true workaholic has a one track mind. Like Simon, his first, second and third love is his business. Nothing can stand in the way of this obsession and relationships are doomed to disaster. It might be better to avoid all the messy problems ahead by simply forgetting romance altogether. After all it's not important to the workaholic.

The workaholic is identifiable by the top phalange of his fingers which are extremely hard, almost like second nails. The phalanges will be even in size but the joints are knotty. The headline would be very straight, the heartline poor and short, probably stopping beneath the second finger of Saturn. The curve of the lifeline around the Mount of Venus would be very shallow, revealing an emotionally cold nature (See Fig 15[a])

Strangely enough although this type of person is likely to be very successful, the success line might well waver on the palm because the subject is prone to wear himself out by working too hard and refusing to take a break.

I would say that the person with such a hand would only find true happiness with another workaholic. They might not see a lot of each other but at least they wouldn't be miserable while apart.

The balanced approach

You don't have to be a complete workaholic to have problems combining business and home life however. Business has a way of encroaching into every area of life and the most devoted partners can find themselves irresistibly drawn in, to the detriment of their relationship.

If your heartline is full and sweeps on to the mount at the base of the first finger of Jupiter and your lifeline swings in a wide curve round the Mount of Venus, you are easily capable of a full, loving relationship. (See Fig 15[b])

The only difficulty is keeping business in check and recognising the problems before they become too great to solve. The best way of doing this is to look for stress on the palm, the tiny criss-cross grilles which reveal undue strain.

When you are under stress at work you tend to spend more time in the office, more time in the pub and more time at home wrapped up in your business problems. All of these things happen, and they put a relationship under great strain yet often the 'guilty' party is quite unaware of it.

When you see stress lines on your palm you'll just have to accept that you are probably neglecting your partner and make a big effort to set aside some time to relax

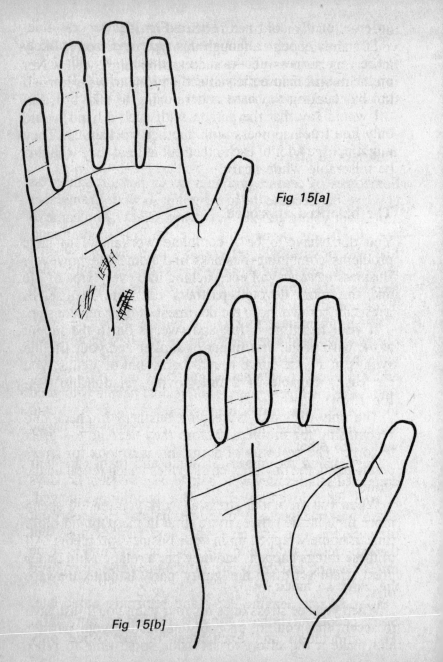

Fig 15[a]

Fig 15[b]

together. If islands have appeared on the success line you've already left it dangerously late and must take a holiday as soon as you can. Immediately if that's feasible. This will help both business and home life. It won't do your health any harm either. (See Fig 15[c])

Partners in stress

Sometimes of course, problems occur not through stress at work, but because the job is going so well. I remember a pleasant young couple, Diane and Clark, who came to see me. It was Diane who made the first appointment. She was obviously upset about something and when I looked at her hand I saw stress grilles around her heartline, showing that her problems were connected with a relationship.

When I mentioned this, Diane told me the whole story. She was worried that her husband was having an affair and she was desperately upset. Apparently they had enjoyed a near enough perfect marriage for several years. Both were intelligent young professional people with good jobs. Money was no problem since both were well paid and neither wanted children, they were completely happy with each other.

They shared the chores at home and thanks to their combined salaries they were able to take frequent holidays abroad. They loved travelling. But then things changed. Clark was unexpectedly made redundant. He wasn't out of work for long and he soon found another post, but the experience shook him. He made up his mind to shine in his new job and this wasn't difficult because he enjoyed the work so much.

Soon he was leaving early and returning home late. Some people might have found it a strain but not Clark. The stimulation and excitement of the office only increased his energy. Clark, of course, was perfectly content. He was too absorbed in his work to notice that Diane was unhappy. Diane for her part could only think of one explanation for her husband's sudden change in behaviour. He must be having an affair. She didn't dare mention the subject in case he admitted everything and said he was leaving.

There was no sign of divorce in Diane's hand so I asked if she could persuade her husband to come and see me. I had a strong feeling that there was no other woman involved but until I met Clark I couldn't be sure.

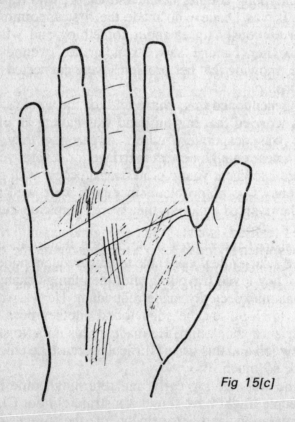

Fig 15[c]

Clark came willingly. His hands revealed a warm, loving personality with a good brain. As I suspected there was no sign of any other relationship but the lines of ambition were very strong. It was obvious that ambition was temporarily blinding him to everything else. There was no stress at all, but then Clark wasn't under stress. It was his wife who was suffering. (See Figs 15[d]) and [e])

I don't usually behave like the Marriage Guidance Council but in this case it was so clear that these two were meant for each other that I couldn't help interfering. I explained to Clark as tactfully as I could that his preoccupation with his job was making Diane lonely and insecure. She was deeply unhappy.

Clark was amazed. Far from being angry he was glad that I'd pointed it out. He loved his wife very much and was horrified that he hadn't noticed how miserable she'd become. That night he went home and talked over the situation with Diane. They agreed that in future Clark would come home earlier whenever possible and they would spend at least one night a week together.

The formula seems to be working. The stress lines have left Diane's hands and the near perfect marriage appears to be back in good shape. The lesson to be learned from this case I realised, is that it's not enough to examine your own hands when trying to keep a relationship on the right lines — you need to look at your partner's hands too. If there are stress lines present for any reason, you need to talk about it.

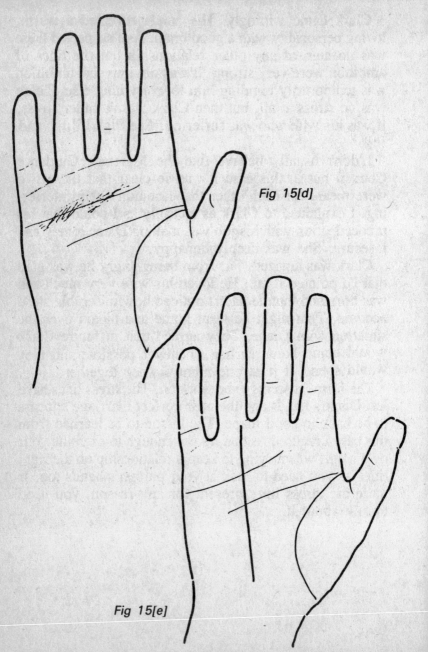

Fig 15[d]

Fig 15[e]